City Planning: A Very Short Introduction

Very Short Introductions available now:

ABOLITIONISM Richard S. Newman
THE ABRAHAMIC RELIGIONS
 Charles L. Cohen
ACCOUNTING Christopher Nobes
ADAM SMITH Christopher J. Berry
ADOLESCENCE Peter K. Smith
ADVERTISING Winston Fletcher
AERIAL WARFARE Frank Ledwidge
AESTHETICS Bence Nanay
AFRICAN AMERICAN RELIGION
 Eddie S. Glaude Jr
AFRICAN HISTORY John Parker and
 Richard Rathbone
AFRICAN POLITICS Ian Taylor
AFRICAN RELIGIONS
 Jacob K. Olupona
AGEING Nancy A. Pachana
AGNOSTICISM Robin Le Poidevin
AGRICULTURE Paul Brassley and
 Richard Soffe
ALBERT CAMUS Oliver Gloag
ALEXANDER THE GREAT
 Hugh Bowden
ALGEBRA Peter M. Higgins
AMERICAN BUSINESS HISTORY
 Walter A. Friedman
AMERICAN CULTURAL HISTORY
 Eric Avila
AMERICAN FOREIGN RELATIONS
 Andrew Preston
AMERICAN HISTORY Paul S. Boyer
AMERICAN IMMIGRATION
 David A. Gerber
AMERICAN LEGAL HISTORY
 G. Edward White

AMERICAN MILITARY HISTORY
 Joseph T. Glatthaar
AMERICAN NAVAL HISTORY
 Craig L. Symonds
AMERICAN POLITICAL HISTORY
 Donald Critchlow
AMERICAN POLITICAL PARTIES
 AND ELECTIONS
 L. Sandy Maisel
AMERICAN POLITICS
 Richard M. Valelly
THE AMERICAN PRESIDENCY
 Charles O. Jones
THE AMERICAN REVOLUTION
 Robert J. Allison
AMERICAN SLAVERY
 Heather Andrea Williams
THE AMERICAN WEST Stephen Aron
AMERICAN WOMEN'S HISTORY
 Susan Ware
ANAESTHESIA Aidan O'Donnell
ANALYTIC PHILOSOPHY
 Michael Beaney
ANARCHISM Colin Ward
ANCIENT ASSYRIA Karen Radner
ANCIENT EGYPT Ian Shaw
ANCIENT EGYPTIAN ART AND
 ARCHITECTURE Christina Riggs
ANCIENT GREECE Paul Cartledge
THE ANCIENT NEAR EAST
 Amanda H. Podany
ANCIENT PHILOSOPHY Julia Annas
ANCIENT WARFARE
 Harry Sidebottom
ANGELS David Albert Jones

Available soon:

For more information visit our web site

www.oup.com/vsi/

Carl Abbott

CITY PLANNING

A Very Short Introduction

OXFORD
UNIVERSITY PRESS

OXFORD
UNIVERSITY PRESS

Oxford University Press is a department of the University of Oxford.
It furthers the University's objective of excellence in research, scholarship,
and education by publishing worldwide. Oxford is a registered trade mark of
Oxford University Press in the UK and certain other countries.

Published in the United States of America by Oxford University Press
198 Madison Avenue, New York, NY 10016, United States of America.

© Oxford University Press 2020

Library of Congress Cataloging-in-Publication Data

Names: Abbott, Carl, 1944- author.
Title: City planning : a very short introduction / Carl Abbott.
Description: New product ed. | New York : Oxford University Press, 2020. |
Series: Very short introduction | Includes bibliographical references
and index.
Identifiers: LCCN 2020016793 (print) | LCCN 2020016794 (ebook) |
ISBN 9780190944346 (paperback) | ISBN 9780190944353 (ebook other) |
ISBN 9780190944360 (epub)
Subjects: LCSH: City planning.
Classification: LCC HT166 .A183 2020 (print) | LCC HT166 (ebook) |
DDC 307.1/216—dc23
LC record available at https://lccn.loc.gov/2020016793
LC ebook record available at https://lccn.loc.gov/2020016794

Printed by Integrated Books International, United States of America

Contents

List of illustrations

Acknowledgments

I thank Scott Bollens for advice about divided cities, Chris Silver for suggestions about Asian planning, and David Gordon for making Edward Bennett's plan for Ottawa and Hull accessible to scholars. My colleagues Jennifer Dill, Sy Adler, Karen Gibson, Laila Seewang, and Federico Perez offered a variety of suggestions. Each of the eight hundred or so scholars who submitted manuscripts to the *Journal of the American Planning Association* while I was coeditor stretched my understanding of the field. Finally, I have learned from my students in the Master of Urban and Regional Planning program at Portland State University, especially as they shared reports and critiques on a multitude of interesting planning initiatives in "Reshaping the Metropolis."

Introduction

Everyone plans. Businesses contemplate markets and products, social service agencies try to improve service to their clients, and politicians calculate their chances for reelection. In the language of urban studies and urban development, however, "planning" refers to efforts to shape the physical form and distribution of activities within cities and regions. The objects of planning are sites and systems—the neighborhoods and places within which we carry on our lives and the networks that link the parts of a metropolitan area into a dynamic whole.

City planning in the twenty-first century is both a practice and a profession. It is a set of goals and sometimes utopian aspirations. It is also the laws and rules that direct the use and development of land. Its history is embedded in regulations and institutions and embodied in the built environment. Past decisions about the management of urban growth have helped to create the vast three-dimensional artifacts that are modern cities. At its best, city planning utilizes technical tools such as subdivision regulations and inclusionary zoning to achieve larger goals set by community action and political debate. It sometimes operates at the broad metropolitan scale of transit networks and air pollution regulations, but it speaks to the experiences of daily life. Can I find an affordable apartment convenient to my job? What can my neighbor do with his vacant lot? Can I get across town in time for my appointment? Can I walk my children to a park, and will they have clean air to breathe? Can I safely bicycle to work? How far do I have to go to buy a loaf of bread?

Let's start by asking what city planners think they do. Britain's Royal Town Planning Institute "champions the power of planning in creating prosperous places and vibrant communities." The American Planning Association "provides leadership in the development of vital communities." The Planning Institute of Australia serves and guides planning professionals "in their role of creating better communities." The Canadian Institute of Planners is a bit more specific: "planning addresses the use of land, resources, facilities and services in ways that secure the physical, economic and social efficiency, health and well-being of urban and rural communities." The *Journal of the American Planning Association* categorizes planning scholarship in seventeen categories that touch nearly every facet of community life. That breadth confirms that formal thinking about the shaping of cities as physical places and social environments calls on the same range of disciplines and approaches that we use for understanding cities themselves, from art and literature through the social and natural sciences.

Whether we call the field "city planning" or "urban planning" in the United States or "town planning" in Britain, it falls in the overlap zone of a messy Venn diagram comprising landscape architecture, civil engineering, architecture and design, geography, history, public policy, public health, real estate, community development, social planning, and environmental management. At the center is a basic concern with the way land is used, especially within relatively compact and dense human settlements, or in the simplest terms, what gets built and where. Planning and planners try to guide both public and private actors. Plans help to decide the location of roads, bridges, sewer lines, and public buildings. They also provide the framework for the development of private property at all scales, from a homeowner thinking of adding an extra room to a corporation funding a massive headquarters complex. The creation and arrangement of the built environment affects every aspect of human activity—where we dwell, where we work, where we spend leisure time, how we move around, who we meet, and who we interact with.

In 2018, the formal associations of planners in four largely English-speaking countries counted seventy-five thousand members: thirty-eight thousand in the American Planning Association, twenty-five thousand in the Royal Town Planning Institute, seven thousand in the Canadian Institute of Planners, and five thousand in the Planning Institute of Australia. The numbers, however, are a fraction of the individuals engaged in city and town planning activities. At the core of the profession are the thousands of local, state, or provincial government employees who staff a sometimes confusing array of bureaus and agencies. In Portland, Oregon, planners work in the Bureau of Sustainability and Planning, the Bureau of Environmental Services, the Parks Bureau, and a semi-independent city economic development agency. They work for suburban municipalities and counties, for park districts, and for regional agencies that deal with public transit, area-wide land use, and port facilities, and for state highway and environmental protection agencies. These public employees support and are supported by another army of volunteers who serve on local planning commissions, advisory committees, design review boards, landmarks commissions, and a myriad of other opportunities for long evening meetings.

Citizens are a second set of actors who engage individually and collectively with formal planning agencies. Homeowners show up at public hearings to praise or protest a proposed building or land use change. Neighborhood groups and community development organizations advocate for the needs and desires of specific groups, whether middle-class homeowners who do not want any change to their nice neighborhood, African Americans protesting housing gentrification and displacement, or small-town residents

3

trying to revitalize their old Main Street or High Street. These folks also come together on behalf of civic goals such as establishing a new park, cleaning up a polluted stream, or preserving a historic building. Taken together, civic organizations and government agencies are community makers who work with the conscious goal of making "better" places. Some concentrate on creating specific urban environments that are more socially harmonious and personally fulfilling than the market usually has provided. Other civic-minded community makers search for ways to make the city and its surrounding region function more efficiently and sustainably.

Interactions between public officials and citizens, whether cooperative or contentious, prepare the canvas for urban development. The amount of preparation varies with scale. Design regulations for a historic neighborhood may dive into the details of acceptable paint colors and replacement windows. Comprehensive plans for an entire city may be more general, with large areas coded yellow for residential, red for commercial, and purple for industrial (the standard colors for land use maps in the United States).

The real estate development industry functions as a third cluster of de facto city planners, filling in the planning sketch with places to live and work. These practical planners see a tract of land, envision it covered with buildings, and try to turn their vision into reality within existing regulations. They put houses on vacant lots, subdivisions and industrial parks on farmland, office towers on the sites of low-rise buildings. They work within the competitive real estate market, but the city they create is unified by common assumptions. In each nation and generation, city builders have created everyday neighborhoods and business districts that reflect prevailing tastes and market forces. Developers draw on the skills of architects, landscape designers, and civil engineers, along with people with planning degrees who understand the bureaucratic complexities.

This introduction to city planning is organized around seven realms of planning: planning as street layout, congestion and decentralization, the conservation and regeneration of older districts, the conflicts that arise from differences of social class and ethnicity, cities and regions, cities as natural systems, and disasters and resilience. Planning has evolved over multiple generations as planners develop new approaches on the foundation of older ideas.

City planning is one facet and contributor to the vast six-thousand-year process of city-making. Townspeople and their rulers have been deciding what to build and where to put it since the days of Ur, Xi'an, and Tikal. However, the distinct field of city planning that dominates contemporary practice took root in early modern Europe, spread with European colonization, developed in response to urban industrialization, and matured as a worldwide practice in the twentieth and twenty-first centuries. Twenty-first-century efforts to shape cities as physical entities and settings for everyday life are a continuation of these past approaches to solving fundamental problems.

A handful of visionaries often dominate narrative histories of urban planning. Since the late fifteenth century, when Leonardo da Vinci proposed to rebuild Milan as a two-tiered city, architects and designers with powerful visual imaginations have generated maps and renderings of cityscapes that claim to promise new and improved lives for their residents. Examples from the 1920s and 1930s such as Le Corbusier's Radiant City of high-rise towers in a park or the diametrically opposite Broadacre City of Frank Lloyd Wright have been technologically feasible if not politically practical. Others, such as the massive self-contained super city Arcologies proposed by Paolo Soleri in the 1960s and 1970s, have been fantastic thought experiments with more influence on science fiction than practical planning. Even at a mundane level, however, the visual or "envisioning" dimension of planning remains important: when a developer is pitching a new project, bankers look at the projected expense and income numbers and everyone else looks at the architect's idealized drawings of the completed project with pastel buildings and plazas populated by happy stick figures.

The visual/visionary dimension of urban planning, with its emphasis on cities as physical objects, exists in tension with an approach that centers on cities as communities with distinct social and political dynamics. Some of the most influential planning ideas have come from social theorists such as Ebenezer Howard, Lewis Mumford, and Jane Jacobs, who relied on words to convey their ideas about the good city. Nothing happens in a modern city without political debates and trade-offs, and planners who approach cities through this perspective recognize a tension between efficiency and equity, between cities as engines for economic exchange and cities as everyday places that work for all residents. The megacorporation Amazon set off a competitive frenzy among American cities in 2017 when announced it was looking for a location for a second headquarters that might employ fifty thousand workers. Economic development planners worked to identify land and incentive packages, but housing planners worried about impacts on housing affordability—one of the worries that led Brooklynites to block Amazon's plans for that borough. Urbanization is a global phenomenon, with more than half of the world population living in cities, and urban planning is also global.

The first university courses in "city planning" were offered in the early twentieth century at the University of Liverpool, Harvard University, and the University of Karlsruhe. Early French programs in architecture and urban engineering combined in 1919 as the Institute d'Urbanisme at the University of Paris. As the number of planning programs in the United States and United Kingdom burgeoned after World War II, graduates and consultants spread Western planning ideas and techniques to universities and government agencies in Europe, Asia, and Latin

America. My home university's doctoral planning graduates teach at their own institutions in Mexico, Egypt, Saudi Arabia, Nigeria, and China. The Global Planning Education Association Network represents more than seven hundred university programs around the world. Consulting firms take planning ideas across continents and oceans, and public officials love to board airplanes to see for themselves how Curitiba or Copenhagen is doing it. Twenty-first-century city planning is indeed an international field and profession.

Chapter 1
Streets and buildings

In 1502, Leonardo da Vinci produced a map of the small Italian city of Imola for the tyrant Cesare Borgia. He depicted the streets in white, individual buildings in brown, and a surrounding moat in pale blue. The map was Leonardo's typically precise contribution to a genre beloved of interior decorators, who adorn the walls of upscale offices with tastefully tinted reproductions of city maps and plans from the Renaissance and Baroque centuries. When we hear "city planning," the first thing that often comes to mind is this sort of a map. The fundamental building blocks of city planning are indeed decisions about the arrangement of streets and buildings, and it is possible to write a history of city planning by arraying and reviewing two-dimensional street maps and plans. To do so is to explore the tensions and contrasts between cities as mosaics of individually held land parcels and cities as physical embodiments of communities and nations.

Europeans plan new American cities

The Spanish invaders who conquered the native empires of Mexico and the Andes found much that was strange, but they found it easy to take over and adapt existing Aztec and Inca cities because their monumental architecture and central focus had similarities to the cities of Renaissance Europe and the classical Mediterranean. Juan Pizarro and his lieutenants moved in on

Cuzco, supplanted the palace of the Inca with a cathedral, left the central plaza, and occupied the other noble houses for themselves. Mexico's conquistadors drew plans and maps of the Aztec capital Tenochtitlan and then rebuilt and adapted it to their own purposes.

Soon, however, the ambitious government in Madrid saw the Americas as the site for new cities to extend and solidify Spanish rule. In 1573, the Spanish Crown issued "Ordinances for the Discovery, the Population, and the Pacification of the Indies." Commonly known as the Laws of the Indies, they are a detailed set of regulations and advices for many aspects of Spanish colonization in the Americas, including town planning. The Spain of Philip II was a bureaucracy that ran on paper, and edicts were intended to make sure that people at the far end of a tenuous line of communication knew what to do.

The most basic instruction was to lay out square blocks with streets at right angles, leaving one or two central blocks for the Plaza Mayor, which was to be fronted by the chief public buildings. The plaza was to be square or rectangular, "in which case it should have at least one and a half its width for length inasmuch as this shape is best for fiestas in which horses are used." Streets were to be laid out at right angles and local officials were to orient the grid to the prevailing winds for good ventilation; in coastal towns the plaza was to face the sea for the same reason. Streets were to be wide in cold climates and narrow in warm ones. These provisions proposed orderly new towns very different from old Iberian cities like Toledo and Seville.

Spain envisioned new cities as tools of an expanding empire. The Laws of the Indies proclaimed: "On arriving at the place where the new settlement is to be founded—which according to our will and disposition shall be one that is vacant and that can be occupied without doing harm to the Indians and natives or with their free consent—a plan for the site is to be made, dividing it into squares, streets, and building lots…and leaving sufficient open space so that even if the town grows, it can always spread in the same manner."

Officials tried to follow the rules even to frontiers of empire. Planted two thousand kilometers north of Mexico City, Santa Fe, New Mexico, grew too slowly to fill out its grid before residents started making changes, but the central plaza still stands, with the Palace of the Governors on one side. The Pueblo of San Fernando de Bexar, the seed for San Antonio, Texas, was a five-block by five-block square, with a two-block plaza faced by a church and royal house. Philip II would have been pleased.

The standards in the Laws of the Indies were appropriate for cities where people moved on their own feet because they emphasized compactness and the primacy of the center. They showed early concern with public health in valuing fresh water and the free flow of air. Founders of new European towns in other parts of North America tried variations on the same principles. A visit to the French Quarter of New Orleans is a time trip to the eighteenth century, when Jean-Baptiste Le Moyne de Bienville laid out a four-by-eleven grid of square blocks along a bend of the Mississippi River, centered on a riverfront Place d'Armes (now Jackson Square) fronted by the church and civic buildings. William Penn instructed his agents in the new colony of Pennsylvania to pick a site for Philadelphia that was high, dry, healthy, and had good moorage in the Delaware River and to make streets "uniform down to the river." Houses were to be sited in the middle of building lots to slow the spread of fires of the sort that had repeatedly ravaged London and create a "green country town." Squares were set off in the city center and at the center of each quadrant—spaces that remain basic to Philadelphia's character. The plan anticipated the American penchant for growth. Streets were unusually wide and Penn made sure that the expansive plan extended from the Delaware to the Schuylkill River "that we might have room for present and after Commers."

Gridded for growth

New York in 1775 was a small city of twenty-five thousand crammed into the lower tip of Manhattan. It had grown by small increments for 150 years as landowners sporadically cut a new street here or staked out a few blocks over there. By the start of the nineteenth century, however, it was closing in on one hundred thousand and had passed Philadelphia as the largest urban center in the Americas north of Mexico City. Landowners and merchants wanted to make continued growth and real estate development easy. The New York state legislature in 1807 authorized three commissioners "to lay out . . . the leading streets and great avenues." Rejecting intricate Baroque street layouts, they chose a right-angled grid as having the greatest "convenience and utility," and they laid across Manhattan the street pattern still in use two centuries later—12 north–south avenues and 155 east–west streets. They admitted that such an ambitious scheme might be "a subject of merriment" but remained convinced that New York would grow into its oversized plan.

The Manhattan grid and Penn's squared-off Philadelphia were models for the new towns and cities that spread over the central and western United States and Canada over the next century. Every new city started small, but founders planned for each to grow through horizontal expansion—an update of the expectation that had been embedded in the Laws of the Indies. These cities of the valleys and plains were private enterprises. Developers, who were sometimes men committed to their new community and sometimes speculators pure and simple, acquired title to a likely site along a river, lakeshore, or projected rail line, surveyed streets and lots, and waited for buyers to make them rich. Townsites were business opportunities and lots were the commodities. Charles Dickens lampooned the notoriously overblown process in his novel *Martin Chuzzlewit*. The gullible hero is enticed to the United States by dreams of getting rich by investing in a new city on the Mississippi River, only to find that "Eden" proves to be nothing but a log shanty in a clearing.

However, satire was no check on ambitious city planning. What was Chicago in 1830, before the city exploded into growth? Sixty empty blocks straddling the fork of the Chicago River. Oklahoma City, a year after the great Oklahoma land rush? A grid of eighty-five blocks on the flat prairie with a railroad running along one side. Ten thousand miles away, plans for new cities in Australia bore a family resemblance. William Light laid out Adelaide in 1837 like an improved version of Philadelphia—a grid of streets with one central and four secondary squares, but buffered by a wide band of parkland. Perth and Melbourne started with waterfront grids that looked a lot like the centers of Cincinnati and Milwaukee.

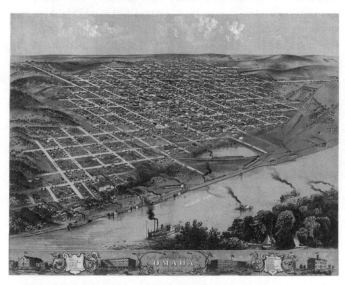

1. The city of Omaha, Nebraska. Omaha was made by both river and rail. This bird's-eye view from 1868 shows the new transcontinental railroad extending west from the Missouri River. Streets extend westward seemingly without end, like the lines in a perspective drawing, suggesting a future of continuous growth.

The rectilinear approach was perfect for towns planned along the tracks of trunk railroads. Congress in 1851 granted the Illinois Central Railroad half the unclaimed federal land adjoining its proposed route as an inducement to build. Four directors of the company, incorporated as the "Associates," purchased land from the railroad where they knew it planned stations (every ten miles or so) and laid out thirty-three towns to a standard plan of forty-five blocks on each side of the rail line, always placing the depot in the middle between Chestnut and Oak Streets. The Canadian Pacific Railway renamed a scattered settlement on Burrard Inlet Vancouver and had one of its engineers lay down a new set of streets for the future metropolis. Alberta's three railroads were responsible for 80 percent of its towns by 1940, using half a dozen standard plans. "Prairie towns all look alike: identical grain elevators, identical banks, identical railway stations, a main street that is called Main Street and a road along the tracks called Railway Avenue," wrote Canadian author Heather Robertson.

The Commissioners' Plan and the popularity of grid plans for new cities small and large have been both lauded and reviled. The great virtue of a street grid is transparency. It is easy to lay out with the most rudimentary surveying skills and easy to navigate—no GPS needed as long as you can count. It makes the transfer of real estate simple because every parcel can be identified by what in effect are *Yes* coordinates, avoiding archaic "metes and bounds" property descriptions based on lines drawn from one landmark to the next. At the same time, a grid is inefficient for cross-town travel, forcing large cities to cut diagonal streets across the squares. Cities often ended up with several grids that do not line up because different developers laid out rival townsites (Denver), tried to match a curving waterfront (New Orleans), or simply followed their own inclinations (Austin). Newcomers to San Francisco discover to their dismay that its grid does not respect the landscape, shooting up and over steep hills in ways that are great for the car chase in *Bullitt* but not for novice drivers. Seattle decided that hills north of the downtown grid were such a nuisance that it washed and dug them away over a thirty-year span, making a gentle walk from downtown to the Space Needle.

Anyone with real estate savvy also knows that gridded cities often contain encapsulated neighborhoods where curving streets are a sign of high status, the result of a changing aesthetic over the nineteenth century. Toward the end of the 1700s, the straight streets and right angles of Edinburgh's New Town represented modernity in contrast to the old, jumbled medieval city. By the mid-1800s, however, romantic valuation of nature prompted developers to adapt streets to natural topography in upscale communities like Lake Forest and Riverside, Illinois. By the twentieth century, a street pattern that varied from the grid signaled a neighborhood or suburb with social aspirations, whether Rosedale in Toronto or Killara in Sydney.

The impact of the New World planning style is obvious when overall street patterns in newer cities are compared to those in Europe. Historic European cities offer the pleasures and frustrations of small-scale incremental growth. Visitors to London, Paris, Rome, or Berlin who stray off the main boulevards discover streets with minds of their own, making a good map absolutely essential and causing endless confusion when street names change from block to block. In contrast, the majority of streets in Mexico City run parallel or at right angles to each other with only occasional diagonals and eccentric curves, reflecting Spanish colonial order. Toronto, Sydney, and Melbourne are also ninety-degree communities whose grids reflect their short histories.

Exported modernity

North America and Australia, along with parts of southern South America and southern Africa, were settler colonies where Europeans and European Americans conquered and displaced indigenous nations and peoples and treated the landscape as open for their own purposes. They could farm as they pleased, and they could build new cities where and how they wished—usually as quickly and simply as possible. In contrast, European imperialists who asserted control over much of Asia and Africa in the nineteenth and early twentieth centuries found long-established and viable societies that they wanted to exploit, not obliterate. They worked when they could through local rulers and elites while imposing their management and planning preferences on established cities such as Tunis and Kolkata. Whereas grid planning in settler societies reduced the abstract differences between one part of a city and another, imperial planning in the eastern hemisphere aimed to make the European part of the city special. Architects from the home country imitated their own capital cities. They designed colonial government buildings around broad plazas with sweeping views and sited new housing for the colonial elite nearby. Colonial administrators built long, straight boulevards that contrasted with the often narrow streets of older districts. At the extreme, they planned and built new squared cities next to the older core, utilizing the design vocabulary that had been remaking such imperial capitals as Budapest and Paris.

France in Morocco and the United States in the Philippines approached colonial city planning from different national planning cultures but with similar results. Hubert Lyautey, who governed French Morocco from 1907 to 1925, approached the cities under his administration with the political philosophy of "association," the French policy that theoretically rejected assimilation and viewed colonial subjects as partners. City planning focused on Rabat as an administrative capital and Casablanca as a commercial center; association manifested as the creation of dual cities where the historic city was carefully preserved while a new city displayed the best of early twentieth-century European modernism. There were—no surprise— impressive public buildings, parks, new residential districts, and long, straight avenues like Casablanca's Boulevard du IVe Zouaves leading to the Place de France (now Boulevard Mohammed e-Hanseli and Place Mohammed V).

While still finishing work on a plan for San Francisco, in 1904 Chicago architect and planner Daniel Burnham accepted an assignment to replan Manila. Only six years had passed since the United States had taken the islands from Spain and only two years since it suppressed a fierce-fought war of independence. He wanted to retain the old walled city but to fill its moat to create a circular park. Adjacent to the old city he located a formal modern civic center whose large open spaces and symmetrical avenues looked a lot like his newly finished proposal for Cleveland. He wanted diagonal boulevards to radiate from the civic center so that "every section of the Capital City should look with deference toward the symbol of the nation's power." An updated Manila could blend the best of two worlds: "a unified city equal to the greatest of the Western World with the unparalleled and priceless addition of a tropical setting."

Imperial Japan also imposed Western planning ideas on an East Asian colony. Japanese planners learned the theory and practice of up-to-date planning through studies in Europe in the early twentieth century and applied them both in Japan and in Japanese possessions. In the 1930s, Japanese officials transformed the small Manchurian city of Changchun into the fast-growing capital for the newly conquered puppet state that they had renamed Manchukuo. The layout of streets, boulevards, and circles and the careful division of residential and commercial districts looked very much like Canberra, the modern capital of Australia that was established in the 1910s.

The imperial makeovers of cities like Casablanca and Manila were modest compared with what the era's grandest empire did to its most prized possession. After the British government in India moved its administrative center from Kolkata to Delhi in 1911, it decided to build a suitable new city adjacent to the historic Mughal capital, not so much respecting as ignoring the older city. New Delhi, as inaugurated in 1931, was a city of magnificent distances. A broad green-lined boulevard leads from a hill with the vast presidential residence (originally the viceroy's palace) past administrative buildings and museums to a hexagonal park. A second circular park, intended as the commercial center, completes a rough equilateral triangle. Smaller circles and diagonal streets create nesting and interlocking polygons. The whole geometric exercise, now engulfed within one of the world's largest metropolitan regions, has a family resemblance to Washington, DC, with its Capitol Hill, National Mall, and many diagonal streets and traffic circles. Britain designed New Delhi to manifest the authority of an occupying power, but the scale was generous enough to allow it to transition to the capital for the world's second largest nation.

Planned capitals

Newly independent in 1947, India inherited a national capital with only two decades of wear. Other newly independent nations have planned and built new capitals from the ground up, an undertaking that requires planning at two scales, starting with the broad question of "where" before concentrating on the more specific question of "what." Deeply political questions about the practical and symbolic functions of a particular regional location come first, linking city planning to regional planning. Choices about the layout, design, and expected size of the new city come second, often the work of outside experts.

There are examples on several continents. Russia was not a new nation at the start of the eighteenth century, but Tsar Peter I radically reconceived it. He founded St. Petersburg on the edge of his empire to anchor Russian conquests on the Baltic and to serve as a gateway for Western culture to influence Russian society; the city grew incrementally with plans by Swiss and French architects.

Other cities deliberately split regional differences. Canberra is neither Sydney nor Melbourne. Ottawa, designated Canada's capital in 1857, when it was still a small frontier town, was midway between the population centers of Ontario and Quebec. It was also safely distant from the potentially hostile United States. Alexander Hamilton and Thomas Jefferson were responsible for the location of Washington, DC. Hamilton got economic concessions for northern states and Jefferson got the new capital located in the upper South. George Washington, who selected the actual site for the District of Columbia, also hoped that a location on the Potomac River would make the new capital the commercial gateway between the Atlantic coast and the American interior; a pleasant section of old canal managed by the National Park Service is what survives from those economic ambitions.

Brasilia, probably the best known among new twentieth-century capitals, had a dress rehearsal. In 1897, the leaders of Brazil's Minas Gerais state cast aside the mining city of Ouro Preto in favor of a state capital that would be suitable for a new era of republican prosperity (Brazil transitioned from empire to republic in 1889). Cidade de Minas—soon to be renamed the future-oriented Belo Horizonte—had a checkerboard of blocks overlaid with diagonals still clearly visible in satellite images. In the 1940s, Mayor Juscelino Kubitschek worked with architect Oscar Niemeyer to enhance the city with parks, lakes, and avenues. In the next decade, during Kubitschek's term as president of Brazil (1956–61), they teamed up on the even grander project of Brasilia, the new national capital on undeveloped land six hundred miles inland from Rio de Janeiro. The goal was a capital that was clean, spacious, and modern, in a location that represented Brazil as a vast nation covering close to half of South America.

The United States was a new nation whose new capital city was intended to embody its independence. Modern Pakistan, Nigeria, and Indonesia have acted on the same impulse. They have found compelling reasons to replace the port city that had been the center of colonial government with a new capital that has suitable buildings and public spaces and few reminders of the colonial era. Islamabad, planned and built in the 1960s in the northern interior of Pakistan, substitutes for the crowded colonial port of Karachi and the historic city of Lahore, which was uncomfortably close to the border of India. Abuja, built in the 1980s and formally made Nigeria's capital in 1991, is in the geographic center of the nation, balancing its major regions and unassociated with the ethnic divisions that led to bitter civil war in the 1960s. Indonesia in 2019 announced plans for a new capital on Kalimantan (Borneo) with a planned build-out population of 1.5 million. The move abandons the "sinking ship" of Jakarta and aims to rebalance the national economy away from Java.

Planned capitals illustrate a persistent problem with master schemes for entire cities, whether they are single maps like Pierre L'Enfant's eccentric plan for Washington, Lucio Costa's bird-in-flight doodle that became the template for Brasilia, or a 280-page master plan that an international team of consultants prepared for Abuja in 1979. It is easier for experts to draw up a comprehensive scheme than it is for a shifting cast of government officials and private individuals to follow it. Governments put public buildings where they were not designated. The US Treasury Building blocks the axis of Pennsylvania Avenue in Washington. The presidential residence in Abuja is off center from where it was planned. Private development follows market opportunities rather than neatly filling in the plan. Abuja has housing developments where they were not intended and more retailing along commercial strips than in the planned compact business centers. The tension between master plans and practice illustrates the theoretical argument of French sociologist Henri Lefebvre that urban space is always the product of an interaction between abstract plans and general regulations, the practical ways in which people conduct their daily lives, and the meanings with which they imbue the places and spaces where they live and work. It is residents who animate plans and bring cities to life.

Chapter 2
The suburban solution

In 1948, the British Ministry of Town and Country Planning issued *Charley in New Town*, an eight-minute cartoon intended to promote new planned communities. It starts with the evils of the city—overcrowding, overbuilding, pollution, social isolation—shown in the darkest tones. The crowds of workers are a flowing black blob, indistinguishable from clouds of coal smoke. The solution for a very perky Charley is to move with his bicycle to a perfectly planned new community where the musical background is cheery, the factories are clean and modern, and the planners have made sure to provide enough pubs.

"Charley" was moving to one of Britain's two dozen "new towns" established between 1946 and 1970. They were designed as semi-independent satellites outside major cities, with populations of up to one hundred thousand, allowing workers to escape the crowded cities. Sweden and Finland built highly regarded new towns, and private developers in the United States tried to follow in the 1970s, with Columbia, Maryland, and The Woodlands, Texas, the only clear successes. The physical results ranged from homey in Hemel Hempstead, England, to avant-garde in Cumbernauld, Scotland, but most of the towns have ended up as hybrids between suburb and satellite.

The New Town program responded to a century of analysis and alarm that viewed industrial cities as health and welfare traps and offered a partial solution to this great city planning problem of the nineteenth and early twentieth centuries. The triumph of city planning in the Atlantic world in the later nineteenth and twentieth centuries was to solve the crisis of congestion with programs of decentralization. The key tools were innovations in transportation, first mass rail transit and then individual automobiles, coupled with mass production of housing. The resulting suburbanized landscape, however, has generated its own problems that cannot be cured with highway building. In a nutshell, suburbanization was the cure for overstuffed cities but also the source of new problems in need of twenty-first-century solutions.

The gospel of decentralization

The industrial city fascinated and horrified the generation that came of age in the late 1800s. Journalists, social workers, and social scientists by the dozen explored and documented the people and neighborhoods of East London, lower Manhattan, and the neglected quarters of Paris, publishing exposes like Jacob Riis's *How the Other Half Lives* and Charles Booth's *Life and Labour of the People of London* (in nine thick volumes). Riis, Booth, and many others reported on the physical problems of overcrowding, inadequate sanitation, and the social problems of embedded poverty and proletarian discontent.

Jack London, the novelist and political radical, spent months in the slums of East London researching *People of the Abyss*, borrowing his title from H. G. Wells's own depiction of metropolitan poverty in *Anticipations* (1901). The American writer turned his eye to the residents of workhouses, street children, the unemployed, and petty criminals and their victims: "I went down into the under-world of London with an attitude of mind which I may best liken to that of the explorer. The starvation and lack of shelter I encountered constituted a chronic condition of misery which is never wiped out, even in the periods of greatest prosperity." In *The Iron Heel*, his dystopian novel of class conflict, he would envision the workers of a future United States trapped in teeming cities while the managers and owners live in nice suburbs and gated communities (it does not turn out well).

Reformers thought planned decentralization was the solution. In 1898, economist Adna Weber argued that "the 'rise of the suburbs' is by far the most cheering movement of modern times…the suburb unites the advantages of city and country" to allow "the Anglo-Saxon race" to escape "hot, dusty, smoky, germ-producing city tenements and streets." The same year, Ebenezer Howard published *To-Morrow: A Peaceful Path to Real Reform*, revised in 1902 as *Garden Cities of To-Morrow*. Howard wanted to use cooperative land ownership to create entirely new "garden cities" that would be separated from London by an agricultural green belt and connected by rail. London would be the metropolitan hub of a great wheel, and garden cities would be dotted around the rim. Howard was enormously influential, and not only on New Towns, partly because of his fetching diagrams but even more because the garden city idea promised a "marriage of city and country" that resonated with Anglo-American culture.

Forty years later, the New York World's Fair of 1939–40 showcased an American variation on Howard's ideas. After trying the Parachute Jump and marveling at the futuristic freeways modeled at the General Motors Futurama, visitors could view *The City*, a film produced by the American Institute of Planners with a script by the urban critic Lewis Mumford and score by Aaron Copland. It opens with happy children playing in a sunny country village before cutting abruptly to the smoke-belching mills of Pittsburgh and rickety houses on the edge of collapse; jumping to anthill New York, where the frantic pace is impossible to bear; and finally coming full circle to a sunny, bucolic suburb full of happy white families. The final scenes were shot at Greenbelt, Maryland,

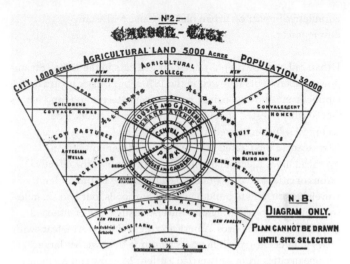

2. Ebenezer Howard's diagram from *Garden Cities of To-Morrow* places a precisely designed, moderate-density community within five times as much farmland. The main-line railroad that serves the community and the wedge shape of the diagram are reminders that Howard envisioned a complete ring of garden cities encircling London and other large cities.

a New Deal attempt at a garden city, and the message was unmistakably the same as sociologist Harlan Paul Douglas's warning in 1923 that "a crowded world must be either suburban or savage."

Rails, roads, and real estate

Two hundred years of transportation innovation, investment, and planning have made suburban nations possible. Cities are compact when people have to get around on foot, whether Periclean Athens or Florence of the Medicis. They spread out when residents can hop on a streetcar or grab the wheel of their Toyota. Rail transit and then road systems have developed through similar overlapping stages, with an interactive and

23

cumulative impact on urban planning and real estate development.

Urban rail began with poky horse-drawn cars in the 1850s. Steam power experiments followed in the 1870s, but cable cars are too cumbersome and expensive except on very steep routes and horses vigorously protested small locomotives on city streets. The technical solution arrived in the 1890s with electrified trams (streetcars in the United States) that take their power from overhead lines. Electrified rail more than doubled the effective radius of cities and thus quadrupled prime development land. Developers rushed to build new neighborhoods four and six miles from city centers, creating new lower-density cities of attached and single-family houses. American cities replaced streetcars with buses in midcentury, while trams continue to crisscross large European cities from Antwerp to Zurich; Moscow and Melbourne had the most functioning track in the early 2020s.

Trams and steam railroads converged on city centers, creating congestion nightmares when wagons, carts, pedestrians, and streetcars competed for the same surface streets. The next step was to take transit off the impassible streets, raising it in the air or burying it. The more expensive but superior subways dive beneath the city core and come up for air toward the end of the line. Although early systems like New York and London developed piecemeal, later subways have been designed as systems with full awareness of the need to connect centers of activity. The desirability of land near stations makes rail lines important, if expensive and long-range, regional planning tools to jump-start new clusters of high-rise offices and housing. Examples range from Bay Area Rapid Transit and Walnut Creek, California, to the district around the Paris Metro stop opened in 1998 to serve the new Bibliothèque National.

Even as rail transit construction has boomed in the twenty-first century, especially in Asia, automobiles keep rolling off assembly lines in the millions. In the United States, each man, woman, and child could ride in the front seat at the same time by 1968, when there was a registered motor vehicle for every two Americans. In turn, automobiles have required dedicated space on streets and roads that multiple users previously shared. Traffic engineers in the 1920s and 1930s developed electric street signals and parking regulations to facilitate vehicular flow. They imposed speed limits. They widened roads and developed the hierarchy of neighborhood, collector, and arterial streets and highways used in the twenty-first century.

Transportation planners also took the same logical step seen with rail transit by removing the heaviest traffic to dedicated limited-access freeways that are simultaneously engineering marvels and traffic sewers. Americans often kick themselves for overcommitting to freeways, but they have not been alone. Italy pioneered with Autostrade in the 1920s; Leeds, England, aspired to be "the Motorway City of the Seventies." The "ideal" metropolitan freeway plan, modified by money, landscape, and politics, resembles a wheel with a set of radial spokes and one or more outer ring roads like London's Orbital, Paris's Boulevard Périphérique, Rome's Grande Raccordo Anulare, and Washington's Beltway. Not to be outdone, Beijing has completed three Ring Road expressways in the twenty-first century.

Pushing new roads through existing cities is always disruptive, with poor neighborhoods bearing most of the costs. Baron Georges Haussmann supervised creation of the grand boulevards of Paris in the 1850s and 1860s by displacing tens of thousands of poor Parisians whose ramshackle housing stood in the way. A century later, American highway engineers picked urban freeway routes that frequently had the same sort of collateral damage, given that poor communities had little political clout, cheaper real estate, and often convenient locations on the fringe of downtowns.

In Britain and the United States, faster transportation made possible new lower-density residential landscapes. Developers in the United States operated on increasingly large scales, with Levittown, New York, and Lakewood, California, well-known prototypes in the first decade after World War II. Middle-class Britons increasingly expected a semidetached house sharing only a single wall with a neighbor or, better yet, a freestanding house, rather than a single unit in a long row. The average single-family lot in American suburbs grew steadily from 5,000 square feet to a quarter acre, and the average size of a new house grew from 1,612 square feet in 1970 to 2,660 square feet in 2017. Changing suburban styles can be seen in the houses picked for television show settings: a pleasant 1920s bungalow in Torrance, California, for Buffy Summers (the vampire slayer), a 1960s ranch style in North Hollywood for the Brady Bunch, and a 1980s McMansion in North Caldwell, New Jersey, for Tony Soprano.

Suburban planning has provided preemptive damage control in the face of the hunger for buildable residential land. Powerful market forces with political support open the way for new housing developments. Planners apply subdivision regulations that try to ensure a modicum of open space, streets that align with the existing road system, and properly engineered sewers and storm drains. A regulatory option for large-scale developments is the planned unit development (PUD), which effectively combines zoning and subdivision regulations to allow flexibility in housing types and in the arrangement of land uses, such as varying lot sizes and grouping open space into larger clusters.

The term "suburb" evokes a low-density residential environment, whether in Philadelphia or on the opposite side of the globe in Perth, but suburbanization in some nations has created sprawling tracts of the sorts of elevator apartments that Americans associate with inner-city public housing. Planners in the Soviet Union, building on the tradition of worker housing in apartment blocks in cities like Vienna and Berlin, opted to house growing urban populations in elevator apartments in *mikrorayons* (microdistricts) on peripheral land. "Greenfield" development avoided the need to work around existing buildings, infrastructure was cheaper, services were easy to provide, and residents were closer to nature—all motivations for American suburbanization as well. Ten- and sixteen-story apartment blocks house two-thirds of Riga's population in such suburban neighborhoods of sometimes windswept concrete slabs, for example. Other Warsaw Pact nations made similar choices. So did centrally planned Singapore, where four of five residents live in Housing and Development Board towers located in satellite clusters with town center facilities and shopping.

A very different example of a shared planning style links American technology districts like Silicon Valley to counterparts in Bangalore and Guadalajara. The industrial park landscape of the San Jose–Palo Alto corridor is a cliché of high-end business and residential development, and the same information age economy has been transforming key centers in the global tech network. Mexican and multinational firms in the later twentieth century created a low-rise suburban manufacturing landscape on the western side of Guadalajara, run by managers and engineers in gated golf course communities that would be at home in Arizona. Large suburban office parks and self-contained tech campuses for software, communications, and biotech companies ring Bangalore. A map of tech firms ringing this leading technology city looks remarkably like a similar map for Austin, Texas. Novelist Douglas Coupland calls these districts futuretowns, sets of "low flat buildings that look like they've just popped out of the laser printer" that are screened by greenery and fronted by enigmatic tech company names. "Futuretowns are like their own country superimposed onto other countries," a point that poor people in India and Mexico might agree with.

Suburbia on trial

British novelist and prime minister Benjamin Disraeli did not like what was happening to mid-nineteenth-century London. "All of those new districts that have sprung up in the last half century, the creation of our commercial and colonial wealth, it is impossible to conceive anything more tame, more insipid, more uniform. Pancras is like Marlyebone, Marylebone is like Paddington, all the streets resemble each other," he complained. "You must read the names of the squares before you venture to knock at a door." Disraeli was unhappy with a very early and mild version of suburbanization. His complaints echoed a century later in Malvina Reynolds's song about "ticky-tacky" houses that "all look the same." Reynolds was not alone. Where advocacy of suburbs and decentralization dominated planning literature in the first half of the twentieth century, the situation turned after 1950 with a sprawling indictment of suburbs and sprawl. If tidy, carefully designed middle-class suburbs of the 1920s and 1930s were fine, not so the mass-produced postwar suburbscape in places such as Daly City, California, where street after street of single-family houses draped over the hills south of San Francisco.

Arguments against sprawl are often aesthetic and ethical. New peripheral landscapes built around automobiles are damned as boring, monotonous, and ugly, marring the beauty of nature and creating "God's Own Junkyard," to cite the title of one angry book. Complaints about "careless," "haphazard," and "wasteful" suburban development carry a moral overtone. If you like carefully planned cities, there is something distasteful about unplanned growth that "messes up" the environment, or at least is not planned within a metropolitan framework. Sprawling suburbs are repeatedly described as unnatural sterile hybrids with the virtues of neither city nor country, the opposite of what Ebenezer Howard hoped from their marriage.

One problem with lambasting sprawl is finding a precise target. For many, sprawl is land development that they don't like, and that's it. Sprawl may imply low density, or a lack of clear centers and edges (what planners call "landscape legibility"), or "leapfrog" urbanization that is scattered and discontinuous. Economist George Galster identifies eight distinct and measurable criteria, including density, continuity, concentration, closeness to a metropolitan center, and diverse land use at small scale. By his calculations, Atlanta is the most sprawling American metropolis and New York the least.

Critics do have numbers to cite when they address the physical impacts of low-density and scattered development. The pattern transfers costs from private to public sector. Peripheral land is relatively cheap, holding down the cost of new housing for individuals, but it is expensive to serve with roads, sewers, water lines, and other utilities that need to extend trunk lines for long distances. Low densities increase costs for emergency services that need to cover large territories and transit agencies that need to operate long bus routes with sparse ridership. Households there spend more time in automobiles than they do in denser areas, with resulting environmental impacts.

The same development pattern stresses natural systems. Patchwork development fragments wildlife habitat, interrupts natural drainage, and disrupts agriculture (suburbanites whose new neighborhoods abut active farms are distressed to find that agriculture can be noisy and smelly). The American environmental movement that gained momentum in the 1970s was in part the work of suburbanites who could observe that postwar subdivisions were destroying the rural landscapes that attracted them in the first place. Traffic jams and air pollution marred overburdened roads that had never been designed for heavy use. Septic tanks in high-density developments leaked sewage that fouled streams. Orange groves fell to the blades of bulldozers. Journalist William H. Whyte summed up: "Sprawl is

The suburban solution

29

bad aesthetics; it is bad economics. Five acres are being made to do the work of one, and do it very poorly. This is bad for the farmers, it is bad for communities, it is bad for industry, it is bad for utilities... it is bad even for developers." Advocates of compact planning now use more sophisticated terminology and have vastly more data at hand, but they make the same basic argument.

As the definitional problem suggests, "suburbanization" is a more comprehensive and neutral term than "sprawl." In the broadest sense, a suburb is a new urban district built further from the city center than older districts. Outlying districts retain their suburban identity when they have a local government separate and independent from the older city, a situation fundamental to the work of city planners who work for local authorities. Aggregate American statistics on "suburbs" depend on this distinction between people living within the boundaries of a central municipality and those living elsewhere within the census-defined metropolitan area. Scarsdale, New York, and the Riverdale neighborhood in the Bronx are similar places to live, but one is suburban and the other is urban according to political boundaries. It is difficult to see any difference when you cross most lines between city and suburbs in a particular metropolitan area, although it is easy to tell the 1940s and 1970s neighborhoods from those built in the present century—Scarsdale is not a twin to Buckeye, Arizona. Given this variety, "suburban ring" or "suburbs" in the plural is a much more useful term than the catchall "suburbia" in most parts of the world.

The social critique of suburbs highlights residents' potential isolation from the full benefits of metropolitan society. The *banlieues* of Paris concentrate working-class residents and people of North African descent, whose tenuous integration into the life of the City of Light triggered rioting in 2005 and whose socioeconomic disadvantages and alienation remain unaddressed. Urban planning choices did not create economic disparities or an ethnic and religious tension, but the postwar decision to build high-rise suburbs for industrial workers has made solutions more difficult. The situation is different in North America, where suburbs have been attracting most new immigrants with their affordable housing, opportunities for entrepreneurship, and clients for ethnic businesses and institutions.

The American critique also highlights the isolation of women in the "sitcom suburb." That sharp edge of criticism, which played a role in fueling second-wave feminism in the 1960s, has been blunted with the rising proportion of working women in the work force (from 34 percent of adult American women working outside the home in 1950 to 57 percent in 2015). However, the separation of large housing estates from the larger city places special burdens on women, who are responsible for most household travel—shuttling children, shopping, and commuting themselves. The planning answers are clear, including better public transportation within suburbs and from suburbs to central city and smaller-scale development with walkable local services.

Back with the old

For most of the twentieth century, the "suburban solution" implied that suburbs were the answer to the problems of overcrowded cities. In the twenty-first century, city planners are more likely to reverse the proposition, seeing themselves as providing solutions for the negative impacts of suburbanization. Good practice and policy include renewed investment in public transit, regulatory limits on outward urban growth, denser development of suburbs, and emphasis on walkable neighborhoods. In effect, the old has become new again, albeit with modern supportive regulations and technologies that seek to make cities livable for people of all ages and social categories.

Everyone who lives in a metropolitan area—Beijing, Sydney, Milan—knows that traffic is terrible and getting worse. Since most people like the convenience of driving, the common demand is to add more freeway lanes. It seems logical that spreading traffic over more lanes will allow every vehicle to move more easily, but it will not work. The technical term is induced demand. The economic principle is simple: make something cheaper or easier and more people will want it. More freeway lanes briefly speed traffic, attracting drivers who had been making do on surface streets and inducing others to make trips that they would otherwise have avoided. Before you know it, congestion is as bad as before. In the 1980s, economist Anthony Downs stated the phenomenon as the law of peak hour traffic congestion: "On urban commuter expressways peak-hour traffic congestion rises to maximum capacity."

Transportation planning tends to be a contest between planners who understand economics and engineers in government highway departments who like to build roads. Because the engineering approach has popular appeal, there are real-world demonstrations of induced demand. The addition of lanes to I-405 in Los Angeles made no dent in travel times. With a $2.8 billion upgrading, Houston's Interstate 10 swelled to twenty-six lanes at its widest but has seen a 30 to 55 percent increase in rush hour travel time. The rapid rise in congestion and increase in travel times in central San Francisco and Manhattan is another example of induced demand. Phone-based ride hailing has been taking customers from taxis, but also from buses, subways, and walking, putting more total vehicles with single passengers on the same set of streets.

The capital-intensive alternative to freeway lanes is new commuter rail, which has been booming around the world. High-capacity transit, usually subways and heavy rail, supports the capital that is already sunk in downtowns and major public facilities, and it promotes concentrated outlying development. It is also a status symbol for nations whose economies have been rapidly catching up with Europe. More than 50 urban rail systems opened in the decade from 2010 to 2019, compared with 105 in the previous four decades combined. Rail expansion in

North America looks impressive, with the expansion of the Washington Metro, Vancouver SkyTrain, and several other systems, until one looks to Asia and Africa, which account for 40 of the 45 newest systems. In 2017, Asian rail transit served twenty-five billion passengers, European systems served ten billion, Latin American systems served six billion, and North American systems four billion. Tokyo, Moscow, and Shanghai had the highest total ridership.

Construction decisions are inherently political because they require allocation of scarce resources. Systems are built incrementally, and the need to secure middle-class support may mean that lines into affluent areas come before lines serving the poorer side of the metropolis, as in Los Angeles. Middle-class white suburbs may veto extensions because they do not want better connections to the poorer central city, as in Atlanta. In contrast, Santiago's decision-makers made it a point of pride to serve poor neighborhoods and job centers with South America's second-largest urban rail system. Meanwhile, Americans assume that middle-class riders who would never deign to ride a city bus will hop on shiny new urban railcars that they catch at a stylish station rather than a grubby street corner.

Alternatives to freeways do not always require billion-dollar investments. Cities can designate dedicated bus lanes, as modeled by Curitiba, Brazil; assure service every fifteen minutes or even more often; and run crosstown as well as radial buses. Protected bikeways and routes are cheap to create, although politically challenging when implemented at the expense of street parking or traffic lanes. North American cities will never be bike-happy Amsterdam or Copenhagen, but they can be more accommodating. Revised subdivision regulations can allow narrower streets to slow automobiles and improve bicycle and pedestrian safety. Suburbs can be retrofitted with sidewalks, a true sign of civilization. Rapid transit stops that are unsafe to access on foot or bicycle lose much of their value. Finally, the economist's strategy to reduce highway congestion is not to add travel lanes but to make driving more expensive through tolling.

European cities lead those in North America. Spain in 2018 drastically limited auto traffic in two square miles in the center of Madrid, with plans for similar actions in more than a hundred other cities. Paris enraged auto owners by removing cars from the lower quays along the Seine and diverting them around major squares like Place de la Republique. Conservative and progressive administrations have together built four hundred miles of bike lanes. From 1990 to 2019, Parisian bike travel increased by ten times, transit use rose 30 percent, and the proportion of trips within the city limits made by automobile dropped substantially. Stockholm, Singapore, and London have successfully adopted the economist's preferred strategy to reduce road congestion by charging them fees to drive into the city centers.

Reducing automobile dependency, with the environmental benefits of reduced local pollution and reduced fossil fuel demand, requires direct transportation actions, as in Paris, and also land use regulations to promote better use of nonautomobile options. At a broad scale, zoning regulations need to support concentrated development around the new rail nodes with upzoning for more intense uses if necessary. The intent is to facilitate "transportation-oriented development" (TOD) with high volumes of residential and commercial space within walking distance of stations. At lower densities, land use plans can promote walkable neighborhoods by allowing duplex and multifamily infill within single-family zones, allowing midrise apartments along streetcar and bus routes, and permitting small commercial/service clusters and strips to scatter within largely residential areas.

Many of these provisions are embraced by the planning movement and ideology of New Urbanism. The Congress for the New Urbanism, which burst onto the scene in the United States in the early 1990s, promotes "complete, compact, connected communities." It prescribes interconnected street grids with small blocks, multiple route choices, and no cul-de-sacs; everyday services within walking range; and a mixture of neighbor-friendly housing styles. Seaside, Florida, the setting for the film *The Truman Show*, is a prototype.

New Urbanism updates the neighborhood unit model that Clarence Perry proposed in 1929. Perry wanted to center neighborhoods on a central park and elementary school, avoid cut-through traffic, and place stores, shops, and churches on busy streets on the edges. Perry was trying to codify some of the planning ideas implicit in the Garden City idea and also found in communities like Bournville, England, a "model village" for

3. The commercial center of Bournville, England, in the early twentieth century had a comfortable village look even though it backed onto a massive chocolate factory. The planned community for factory workers and white-collar families has retained its character for a century and a quarter.

workers at the Cadbury chocolate factory that was being surrounded by the growth of Birmingham.

New Urbanist principles can be operationalized in the goal of creating neighborhoods that allow residents to substitute walks and biking for driving (the shorthand is the "five-minute" and "fifteen-minute" neighborhood). Walk scores that calculate distances to shopping, services, and public facilities are now available for every urban address in the United States. Many suburbs have been trying hard to develop their own downtowns and community centers and modify the image of SUV paradise. The Shanghai Master Plan for 2035 proposes to expand green areas so that 90 percent of the residents are within a five-minute walk of public open space and sets the goal of "a fifteen-minute community living circle" so that 99 percent of its residents will have a full range of community services within a fifteen-minute walk.

A fifteen-minute or twenty-minute city is equitable and healthful. When urban areas require automobile trips for every activity, children, the elderly, poor people, and people with physical or mental limitations are all at a disadvantage. So are women, who shoulder the majority of household driving. To the degree that urban planning and design can encourage walking and bicycling, they have positive impacts on health. Indeed, the goal brings city planning full circle. It had origins in concerns about public health—the need to improve sanitation and air quality, mitigate disease, and create more salubrious housing—but diverged as a profession from civic engineering and public health over much of the twentieth century. The growing emphasis on cleaning air, fighting global warming, and improving individual health by reducing reliance on individual automobiles is an important step in reuniting the health and planning professions.

Chapter 3
Saving the center

Teenagers were playing ping-pong in a corner of the striking new Library of Birmingham when I visited in 2016. Britain's second city opened its Central Library in 2014, bringing new life to somewhat sterile Centenary Square. The library bustles with students from the city's many ethnic communities working on assignments, adults exploring career opportunities, visitors enjoying the view from two rooftop decks, and, of course, traditional patrons looking for books. Birmingham, long known as an unglamorous industrial powerhouse, outgrew its central library at the same time that the old building was sitting in the way of an expanding business district. Moving the library promised to open one development opportunity and possibly prime the pump for development elsewhere. In a city with some problematic postmodern architecture, the hip new building has become one of the more popular British visitor attractions outside London.

Birmingham's library is a sign of the continuing—or sometimes renewed—vitality of city centers. Multifunctional centers have been part of the fabric of Western cities for a century and a half. Philadelphians go to Center City, Chicagoans know the Loop and North Loop, and Manhattan has Midtown. Other American cities have "downtowns," and the people of Britain can enjoy their "city centres" and "High Streets." These central business districts, or CBDs in planning jargon, grew from disreputable commercial

4. The Library of Birmingham helps to create an arts-oriented center for the English city. Investment in cultural institutions—museums, theaters, libraries, universities—has been common strategy for cities around the world.

waterfronts when webs of new commuter rail lines, trolleys, tramways, and subways converged at city centers between 1850 and 1930. Every new line reinforced the advantages of centrality. They carried the throngs of shoppers and workers who made department stores and high-rise office districts economically viable. Interspersed were theaters, restaurants, specialty retailers, hotels, government buildings, museums, and concert halls, all sited to be accessible to the greatest number of customers and clients.

Le Bon Marché in Paris is usually credited as the first department store; Emile Zola immortalized the Parisian department store and "the poetry of modern activity" in *Au bonheur des dames* (to the delight of the ladies) in 1883. A generation later, Sinclair Lewis caught the essence of the classic American downtown when he opened his novel *Babbitt* (1921) with a view of a fictional city (that he modeled on Cincinnati and Minneapolis) with a distant view of its new downtown: "The towers of Zenith aspired above the morning mist; austere towers of steel and cement and limestone, sturdy as cliffs and delicate as silver rods." He followed with a view from the street of "the thickening darting traffic, the crammed trolleys unloading, high doorways of marble and polished granite."

To find the early twentieth-century CBD, you looked for train stations. Central London sits inside a ring of trunk line stations serving different quadrants of Britain—Waterloo, Victoria, Euston, King's Cross, Liverpool Street, and half a dozen others. A ring of six railroad stations for intercity passengers bounded the Chicago CBD. Six major stations similarly surrounded the heart of Paris. The still-busy downtown of Missoula, Montana, stretched along Higgins Avenue between the Northern Pacific and Chicago, Milwaukee, and St. Paul railroad stations.

Blight and urban renewal

Downtown ran into trouble in the 1950s. Planners and real estate experts in the decade after World War II had continued to assume that CBDs were the unitary centers of their urban regions. Comprehensive plans for American cities such as Dallas and Cincinnati took a strong CBD as a given that simply needed enhancement with a new civic center or bypass highway. "Downtown continues to hold its position as the gathering place of America," stated the Urban Land Institute in 1954, "the center of business and finance, the center of shopping on its most lavish scale, the center for theaters and culture." Then reality hit and planning ideas changed seemingly overnight. Investors and officials woke to the problems of obsolete office buildings and competition from suburban malls with their free parking. Locally based business groups like Downtown St. Louis, Inc., and the Indianapolis Civic Progress Association sprang up to press city governments for action.

The favored tool in the United States was Urban Renewal. Written in lower case, "urban renewal" in the United States and "urban regeneration" in Britain became generic terms for core area redevelopment. Urban Renewal in capital letters was a federal program authorized in 1954 and expanded in 1959 that made funds available to cities that demonstrated that they had a "workable program" to clear and redevelop underutilized land. City planners identified fringe areas where buildings were dilapidated and where poor people lived in boarding houses and cheap hotels. Following the established theory of urban ecology, which understood the geography of cities as a series of concentric rings around a center, they assumed that the areas surrounding downtown were "zones in transition" with low-value real estate. Redevelopment initiated by local governments would simply facilitate a natural process, removing socially marginal residents and dilapidated buildings.

Urban renewal gained the approval of the US Supreme Court in 1954. The "takings clause" of the Fifth Amendment, which prohibits the federal government from taking property without just compensation, had long allowed condemnation and acquisition of private land for obvious public purposes like bridges or schools, but a Washington, DC, business owner challenged the right of the District of Columbia Land Redevelopment Agency to take his property and transfer it to another private entity. In *Berman v. Parker*, the court sided with the city, unanimously affirming that private land could be taken for the broad public purpose of eliminating blight. A half century later, Berman was the precedent for the highly controversial *Kelo v. City of New London* (2005), which extended the principle to allow forced acquisition of a nonblighted house to support the expansion of a specific pharmaceutical company.

Urban renewal was targeted rather than comprehensive. Resources were inadequate to remake and modernize the entire downtown fringe, so city planning departments and urban renewal agencies zeroed in on areas that combined extreme unsightliness, poor people, and redevelopment opportunities. Their implicit and sometimes explicit goal was to sanitize the city core and make sure it was comfortable for middle-class shoppers, workers, and residents. They gathered social data, inventoried properties, and prepared maps that identified blighted areas with splotches of red or black ink. The city or its redevelopment arm acquired and cleared land, upgraded streets and utilities, and transferred land to private hotel, apartment, and office developers and to land-hungry hospitals and universities. They also built convention centers, sports arenas, stadiums, civic centers for state and local governments, and occasionally low-income housing. Atlanta cleared land for the expansion of Georgia State and Georgia Tech universities, an auditorium and convention center, new housing, and a new stadium on the edge of downtown with lots of surface parking to lure the Braves baseball team from Milwaukee. Mayor Ivan Allen claimed in 1966 that "Atlanta is riding the crest of a four-year wave of progress unmatched in the history of any American city."

European redevelopment was more varied. Cities that had suffered severe wartime damage, such as Rotterdam, required wholesale reconstruction of their central areas. After decades of debate, Stockholm decided in 1962 to clear much of its historic

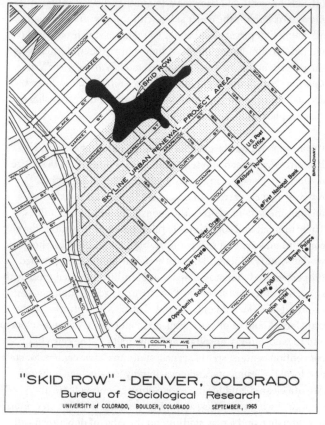

5. In 1965, researchers at the University of Colorado mapped the Larimer Street district, Denver's historic skid row, as an area of urban blight with the unmistakable image of an ink stain. Much of the district was cleared in the Skyline Urban Renewal Project, the extent of which is indicated with small dots.

center to create wider streets, parking, and new commercial buildings. Other cities stepped more cautiously in remaking the thick fabric of historic centers. The French government, to considerable controversy, cleared the historic Les Halles market for an ugly shopping mall but chose to promote a new modernist office district—La Défense—six miles from the heart of Paris at the end of the grand axis through the Arc de Triomphe. An "edge city" long before journalist Joel Garreau would coin the term to describe American suburban office clusters, its sleek towers provided the backdrop for Jean-Luc Godard's science fiction film *Alphaville*. Smaller cities did not want to miss out; Aylesbury grew rapidly with overspill from London in the 1950s and 1960s. To the dismay of traditionalists, it responded by modernizing its core with a new shopping center to supplement the High Street, a ten-story tower that combined local government offices and a bus station, and new space for the country's second-largest Woolworth's.

Planners and politicians in Bogota were just as interested as Americans in displacing unruly and marginal residents and remaking their city center for the middle class. Following rioting in 1948, they authorized the city's first high-rise buildings and cleared slums by pushing wide avenues through working-class districts, as Haussmann had done in Paris a century earlier. In the 1980s and 1990s the city cleared "dirty," "sordid," and "congested" tenements for middle-class apartment towers, replacing unwanted density with good density. International planning consultants and the example of Singapore played important roles in shaping and justifying the urban regeneration projects.

The Jane Jacobs revolution

Five years before Ivan Allen wrote so enthusiastically, Jane Jacobs shook the foundations of urban planning with *The Death and Life of Great American Cities* (1961). Jacobs was a well-connected architecture journalist who used her writing skills to explain what "planners" (her catchall term for everyone who shaped the physical form of cities) had been getting wrong and what to do about it. The problem was massive, top-down projects, including most examples of urban renewal as well as freeway construction.

The answer was to support the natural social fabric of the city and enhance the pedestrian realm. She popularized ideas that became commonplace—the importance of active sidewalks, the need for short blocks and neighborhood parks, the value of affordable old buildings for new businesses, the difference between "gradual money" for neighborhood improvement and "cataclysmic money" that upended and transformed neighborhoods. Her critique was both aesthetic and ethnographic, and the mantras were "small scale" and "diversity."

Jacobs took on all comers, from Ebenezer Howard and Le Corbusier to contemporary architects, developers, and engineers. Despite her references to other large cities, Jacobs aimed most directly at Robert Moses, New York City's king of park, bridge, and expressway development, with whom she had already fought over the future of Greenwich Village. Even for smaller cities with no equivalent of the village, her thinking about the everyday experience of downtowns and neighborhoods made Jacobs the most influential English-language commentator on city planning in the second half of the twentieth century. With anecdotes and examples, she offered an accessible version of the argument that sociologist Michel de Certeau would later make about the difference in viewing and planning a city from the top of a skyscraper and observing how residents use and adapt it day to day.

Ciudad Guayana, an industrial city planned from scratch in the interior of Venezuela, illustrates the problems with top-down "professional" planning. Sited where the Caroni River meets the Orinoco, the new city was part of an ambitious national development policy. The planning team came from Harvard and MIT and largely worked out of offices in Caracas a full day's drive away. They were architects, urban designers, and economists. With the best intentions, they prepared a static plan for a modern future city without paying attention to the needs and expectations of people already living in the area. The brightly colored land use patterns on their maps did not always reflect reality on the ground—their blue rivers were actually muddy brown and green parks and neighborhoods more often were dusty tan.

Twenty years after the project started there was not one city but two, one with lonely clusters of office and apartment towers for the officials and corporate managers and a second for the workers who kept things going. Critic Lisa Peattie, an anthropologist attached to the planning team, characterized the contrast as the view from the barrio versus the view from the design studio. Or, as one Venezuelan economist put it, "no matter how well they plan it, people keep moving in and messing it up."

Jacobs was not alone in critiquing large-scale redevelopment planning. Market-oriented critics argued with considerable accuracy that urban renewal was driven by politics rather than market realities, pointing to cities where large cleared tracts sat vacant because officials had overestimated the demand for downtown real estate. Social critics simultaneously argued that targeted neighborhoods were viable communities and "urban villages" rather than dysfunctional slums. The blocks south of Market Street in San Francisco were easy to label as substandard with their single-room-occupancy hotels, cheap bars, second hand stores, and repair shops, but they were also home to a stable population of older residents who were no longer in the labor force. Residents and community activists fought redevelopment for two decades before the area upscaled into trendy SOMA. Down the coast, Dodger Stadium opened two miles from Los Angeles's Pershing Square in 1962. It is an enjoyable place to watch baseball on a summer evening, but few fans remember that it sidelined plans to use the site for public housing and displaced an established Mexican American neighborhood.

Jacobs helped downtown planners rediscover the importance of active streets and to see their CBDs as sets of subdistricts rather than single places and revaluing older parts of the cityscape.

Suburbs had multiplex cinemas, but downtown had nightlife and arts districts with theaters, concert halls, and museums. Suburbs had cookie-cutter strip malls, but downtowns had traditional routes for holiday parades. In formal planning, the emphasis shifted toward architectural design standards, preservation of historic buildings, programs to allow larger or taller buildings in return for public amenities such as plazas, and similar approaches that treated downtowns as visual experiences. Chicago's 1981 Comprehensive Plan mentioned leisure-time activities first, cultural institutions second, and offices third. San Francisco's 1985 Downtown Plan was a climax of aesthetic planning that gave half its space to issues such as historic buildings, open space, and promoting an interesting skyline through design review by a panel of experts.

Many cities decided that their natural downtown needed extra attractions. In the later 1970s and 1980s developer James Rouse turned from suburban malls to pioneer the "festival marketplace," repurposing historic buildings such as the Faneuil Hall Market in Boston and building Harborplace in Baltimore. Their impressive success triggered imitations in scores of other cities, usually involving the same sort of public/private partnership that had been tried with urban renewal. An extreme example is Horton Plaza in San Diego. It is a contrived environment, dropped onto half a dozen downtown blocks, that draws visitors into a deliberately confusing shopping mall with multiple levels, bridges, and curving corridors decked in Mediterranean pastels as a "fun" alternative to the gray office buildings around it. It was largely vacant by the end of the 2010s, an urban fad no longer fashionable. The parody climax is the artificial downtown of CityWalk, an enclosed promenade of restaurants, shops, and theaters constructed next to the Universal Studios theme park just off the 101 freeway in the Hollywood Hills. It is an ersatz Times Square for tourists—and has a clone in Osaka.

There are only two CityWalks, but many cities have much more commendably matched Birmingham's new library. Chicago was a leader. After protracted debate, the city picked a location on the shabby southern edge of the Loop and opened the Harold Washington Library in 1991, helping to catalyze investment in the old rail-oriented/industrial blocks south of Congress Street. New libraries, like museums and concert halls, are free-standing opportunities for cities to demonstrate their sophistication. Amsterdam, Alexandria, and Helsinki have new libraries. Urban boosters know that engaging star architects for public buildings encourages cultural tourism and brands their city as progressive. Vancouver and Salt Lake City both hired Moshe Safdie, Denver signed Michael Graves, Minneapolis commissioned Cesar Pelli, and Calgary called on the design firm Snøhetta. Architectural theorist Rem Koolhaus put his idiosyncratic twist on Seattle's central library. With striking mesh exterior and counterintuitive arrangements of books and escalators, it has gained the city extra architectural credit for coolness—not to mention four and a half stars as a tourist attraction on Yelp. China's third-largest city presents its huge new library as "the symbol of Guangzhou, an open inclusive city that is brimming with vitality."

Birmingham has ordered all the courses off the urban regeneration menu. Festooned with roundabouts in British style, a multilane highway loop encloses an urban core of roughly two and a half square miles where new developments mix with the nineteenth-century city. Newer multilevel shopping malls cater to mass-market and upscale shoppers. The library shares space with the Birmingham Repertory Theatre, is a very short walk from a convention center with a superb symphony hall, and steps down to a complex of restaurants, offices, housing, and an aquarium along the historic canals. On the other side of the retail core are restored performance spaces, Aston University, and Birmingham City University. A new light rail line crosses pedestrian-only shopping streets (an idea that works much better in Europe and perhaps Australia than the United States). Central Birmingham has an awkward topography and convoluted street pattern, and not all of its old and new pieces work together, but it is a good example of a city that was a municipal leader in the nineteenth century trying the tools of contemporary planning to position itself for the twenty-first.

Downtowns for global cities

When the Baltimore Orioles opened Camden Yards baseball park adjacent to the Baltimore CBD in 1992, they reversed a generation-long trend of building suburban ballparks in seas of parking. Denver, Cleveland, Seattle, Cincinnati, San Francisco, Detroit, and San Diego (two blocks from a new library) have followed. The goals are to enhance downtown's entertainment draw and to repurpose underutilized industrial land. The first purpose has extended the main planning thrust of the 1980s and 1990s. The second has looked to the present century and the need for more opportunities for real estate investments to make cities globally competitive in a neoliberal economic regime of highly mobile business investment and activity.

From the 1950s through the 1980s, CBD planning aimed first to better position the core to compete within its metropolitan region against regional retail malls and "edge city" office clusters and second to compete with other cities within its regional or national economy—Charlotte with Atlanta, Calgary with Edmonton, Melbourne with Sydney. With the ever-growing importance of financial and business services in an information economy, larger cities have begun to plan as if downtown is less the focus for an individual metropolis than a networked node of activity that battles for position within the global webs of the postindustrial economy. Economic development officials study their city's scores in global hierarchy lists prepared by consulting firms, journalists, and academics. The rankings weigh upscale amenities, air connections, and the strength and reach of the finance–management complex. New York, London, Paris, and

Tokyo compete for top spots. Sydney, San Francisco, Madrid, and Milan are members of a second tier. And the rich get richer: Montreal struggles to keep pace with Toronto. Osaka has a "Tokyo problem."

Urban renewal planning targeted specific problem areas. Comprehensive downtown planning in the 1970s and 1980s was more like a systematic physical exam followed by a recommended program of diet, exercise, preventive medications, and a bit of elective surgery. When the contemporary downtown has been most economically successful, however, it has needed more space and more real estate investment opportunities, leading cities and their private partners to eye derelict or outmoded industrial areas on the edge of the core, particularly rail yards and waterfronts with large chunks of easily assembled land. These areas, where land acquisition and displacement costs are low, are prime locations for new offices, upmarket housing, and recreational amenities to attract global corporate offices, financial and professional services, and well-educated members of the white-collar elite.

The close connection between urban regeneration planning and private interests is a reminder that the promotion of economic growth through more efficient and intense use of land has long been central to city planning. The new downtowns are intended to serve what neo-Marxist analysis calls the secondary circuit of capital, in which money made from producing raw materials and turning them into manufactured goods seeks higher returns through real estate development and speculation. Because capital in the secondary circuit is footloose—not tied to specific resources or locations—cities have to run hard to remain as attractive as their competitors.

London's Docklands is a prototype for this postindustrial expansion. By the 1970s, a huge expanse of docks and warehouses on the north bank of the Thames in east London was surplus and derelict. The British government created the London Docklands

Development Corporation (1981–98) as a broad redevelopment agency. It built the Docklands Light Railway direct to the City of London and marketed land to major developers. Canary Wharf, the site of London's then-tallest building, was first a showpiece and then a financial disaster during a real estate recession in the early 1990s. It then recovered as a centerpiece for what has become a second London financial district. The "neighborhood" serves well-paid professionals but not the working-class families who had once made their living at the wharves and warehouses.

Other cities have pursued the same strategy. Buenos Aires transformed the derelict docks of Puerto Madero into an upscale district with international cachet. Melbourne's own Docklands, west of the city center, has developed in fits and starts. The special state agency VicUrban and then the city cut the district into parcels to attract individual developers. As often with urban redevelopment in earlier decades, it has taken some years for market demand to catch up with ambitious plans for corporate offices and housing for ten thousand residents going on twenty thousand–plus.

Docklands stories are reminders that comprehensive plans are agendas for both public and private action. The public sector can create parks, build affordable housing, and improve transportation systems. The private sector has to build the offices, retail centers, and private housing that fill out the plan, which usually means crafting public–private deals that match public incentives to private capital one parcel at a time. The municipality might agree to improve or to vacate a street, to award a height bonus, or to rezone a marginal parcel. Activity in the twenty-first century may use new buzzwords ("creative quarter") but it looks a lot like the previous era.

The central characters in English novelist Margaret Drabble's *The Ice Age* (1977) are real estate developers. On one visit, the more sophisticated developer tours another around "Northern town centers that he had developed [and] showed him the shops, offices, described deals with councils and triumphs over competitors." Four decades after publication of the novel, the city council of a northern, or at least midlands, city published Building a Better Nottingham in 2018 with the goal "to make sure the city compares with the very best of European regional capitals." The report describes several core districts, highlights their amenities, and invites investors—real-life versions of Drabble's characters—to contact the city's regeneration team about "opportunity sites" in the city center and adjacent neighborhoods.

One common goal in new central districts is the desire to create spaces for public use—squares, plazas, waterfront promenades. Sometimes they hit the jackpot, as with Chicago's Millennium Park, popular equally with tourists, office workers, and suburbanites on safari. Other amenity projects raise concerns. New York's High Line converted an elevated rail line into a linear park. It is an outstanding design achievement that struggles to appeal equally to every New Yorker. Success is also a bit subdued at Salford Quays in Manchester, another docklands do-over with the normal mix of housing and office towers, shopping, new tram line (of course), and blandly pleasant promenades along the old ship basins. The development is part of Manchester's effort to fall no further behind London, a tough task for a city that just makes the top one hundred global cities while chasing number two.

Whether playing catch-up like Manchester or growing explosively like Shanghai, cities find it easy to pursue investment and global status by planning city centers for the upper fifth of their residents and forgetting the historic role of downtowns as common ground. Downtowns at their best can be everybody's neighborhood, shared space for people of different backgrounds and from different parts of the metropolis. In the early and middle twentieth century their department stores and theaters served the entire city. Their streets hosted patriotic and community parades, lovingly spoofed in the

"Twist and Shout" scene in the great Chicago film *Ferris Bueller's Day Off*. While planners try to position their cities in the global economy, they should keep in mind that central public spaces are vital to civic life. From London's Trafalgar Square to Plaza Italia in Santiago, Chile, great cities have accessible places for democracy to happen. The United States needs the National Mall and adjacent parks for demonstrations for all political causes. Wenceslas Square in Prague in 1989 helped to make history; so did Tahrir Square in Cairo in 2011.

Core district planning also shows the reach of a widely shared planning vocabulary—modernist renewal projects in the 1960s in both Sweden and Canada, twenty-first-century efforts to craft amenity-rich cityscapes from Singapore to San Francisco. Networks of architects, engineers, and planning consultants with international practices spread common ideas. So do international conferences and organizations and the global influence of western European and North American planning education. The current regime of information exchange is a greatly expanded version of steamship travels in which, for example, Americans learned new ideas about urban sanitation from Britain, land use zoning from Germany, and civic design from continental capitals. American architects Daniel Burnham and Charles McKim and landscape architect Frederick Law Olmsted Jr. spent a pleasant summer in 1901 visiting Paris, London, Vienna, Budapest, Venice, and Rome before buckling down on their very successful plan for making Washington a worthy capital. In the twenty-first century the ubiquity of affordable air travel means that delegations of officials and civic leaders who hopscotch around the globe looking for best practice examples can emulate Burnham in a long weekend rather than a leisurely summer—more information exchange, but perhaps less depth. Nevertheless, the result is an international design and planning vocabulary that is shaping city centers on every continent in the interests of global business and the neoliberal economy.

Chapter 4
Contested communities

Concealed within the captivating sketches of development schemes and the technical language of planning regulations is the problem of bias in city planning. Planning is implemented by people with economic or political power, and it has tended to serve the interests of those with an economic stake in urban real estate—downtown investors, suburban builders, and homeowners—and those with the privileged social positions that come with being white, male, well educated, or well off. The results can be as blatant as routing a Miami freeway to create a barrier between white and black neighborhoods or as subtle as designing public plazas without considering women's safety concerns.

Land use and development lie at the heart of local politics. City planning is inherently political, because it allocates the benefits and costs of urban growth and urban living. The German and Soviet armies at Stalingrad battled block by block for enormous stakes. Developers, homeowners, community activists, and municipal officials battle block by block over seemingly petty disputes that can have large implications for social and economic equity. Land use zoning ordinances and by-laws look definitive, but they are actually debatable. They come with provisions for conditional uses, things that are not automatically allowed but are permissible with certain stipulations, and with the possibility of variances, which are explicit exceptions to the rules. Zoning may also come with the bonus of additional allowed square footage that rewards good developer behavior like providing extra open space.

The result is retail politics in which competing interests lobby planning boards and town councils over issues like allowing an apartment building to exceed a height limit, agreeing to a duplex in a neighborhood of single houses, or permitting a house to be located too close to a property line. The details are different but the basic dynamic is similar in Bogota and Boston. Novelist Margaret Drabble nailed the importance of insider knowledge in *The Ice Age* (1977). One of her characters is trying to put together a project in South London, and one of his colleagues "knew many of the developers' architects and their way with zoning boards....The council liked Rory's architect's plans, and the old buildings came down."

Planning for the middle class

Nineteenth-century European and North American cities were jumbled places. Land owners did their own thing, erecting buildings small or large, cheap or elegant, one lot at a time or several blocks under a single scheme. Uses mixed together, stables behind mansions, shops beside stables, shanties behind shops, factories in the middle of aspiring neighborhoods. There were distinct commercial districts and tracts devoted to fine residences, but there was always the threat that an undesirable new development or neighbor would undercut property values. The resulting hodgepodge of housing types and business uses posed a financial and social threat to residents of more upscale neighborhoods, who wanted their pleasant house and quiet lifestyle to be matched by their neighbors. The result has been a century and a quarter of evolving efforts to restrict and direct the development and uses of urban land in ways that preserve the value of higher-status neighborhoods and prime commercial locations.

Property developers and owners can try to avoid government regulation entirely by restricting land uses through private agreements. In some instances, developers define an apparently public space as private by never ceding it to public ownership, as with private streets in St. Louis and private, gated parks and squares in London. Many subdivisions in the United States in the early twentieth century came with restrictive covenants that applied to every lot, even as it passed from one owner to the next. A covenant typically specified permissible uses, set building standards, and, notoriously, excluded nonwhite buyers and renters. In one example from thousands, the Alameda Park neighborhood in Portland, Oregon, advertised itself as "a fitting homesite, a golden investment" and "part of the largest restricted residence section upon the Pacific Coast." Specifics included minimum values for new houses ($2,500 to $3,500), twenty-foot setbacks from property lines; no business uses except on a few lots at the corners of the plat; no apartments, hotels, or stables; and "likewise no people of undesirable colors or kinds." The US Supreme Court declared that racially restrictive covenants are legally unenforceable in *Shelley v. Kraemer* (1948), although the language is still present in many deeds.

Real estate covenants occasionally added Jews to the forbidden list by including persons of "Semitic descent or blood" along with other undesired groups. This was less common than anti-black and anti-Asian restrictions, and some states, such as Minnesota in 1919, directly disallowed restrictions based on religion or creed. The private real estate market, however, embedded anti-Semitism in its everyday practice. Into the 1960s, residents of places as superficially different as Westchester County, New York, and Dayton, Ohio, knew which neighborhoods and suburbs were open and which were not.

Covenants continue in the form of the CCRs, or covenants, conditions, and restrictions, that apply to "common interest developments" that may range in size from a set of six row houses, to a condominium tower, to a massive resort and retirement community like Sea Pines Plantation in South Carolina. Homeowners associations enforce rules about such concerns as exterior paint colors, collect fees to maintain common areas, and often provide services and recreational facilities, partially substituting for local government and shifting costs from tax payments to assessments. Some communities use these agreements to limit residents to older adults. In recent decades, many such communities have been built inside walls and gates in the American South and Southwest and countries with a fast-growing middle class such as India and Brazil (where the enclosed housing estate is known as *condominio fechado*). The result is a patchwork of "privatopias" where the self-interest of individual sorting and group separation within the private market replaces the shared ground and interests of the public realm.

Privatopias have begun to show up in American fiction. John Barth's *The Development* (2008) offers both wry and acerbic observations on the white-collar seniors who have retired to gated "Heron Bay Estates" on Maryland's Eastern Shore. Their motivation for semi-isolation is exclusionary comfort. T. C. Boyle's *The Tortilla Curtain* (1995) is a lacerating exploration of privatized real estate as a tool for ethnic separation in Los Angeles. The homeowners of "Arroyo Blanco," an upscale subdivision high up Topanga Canyon, decide first to install gates to their private development, then to build a wall to keep out "coyotes," the community shorthand for frightening humans as well as animals. A local real estate agent describes fears of racial change that still sound familiar: "The invasion from the South had been good for business to this point because it had driven the entire white middle class out of Los Angeles proper and into the areas she specialized in: Calabasas, Topanga, Arroyo Blanco...all the smart buyers had already retreated beyond the city limits....There had to be a limit, a boundary, a cap, or they'd be in Calabasas next and then Thousand Oaks and on and on up the coast until there was no real estate left."

Formal land use zoning is the alternative to ad hoc private regulation. US cities in the later nineteenth century experimented with social zoning (e.g., designating a Chinese district in San Francisco) and with "brick ordinances" that required fire-resistant masonry or brick construction in the urban core (often enacted after devastating fires, as in Denver in 1863 and Chicago in 1871). More than a dozen Southern cities tried explicit racial zoning in the 1910s, taking inspiration from South Africa's Native Lands Act (1913), which divided that nation: in 90 percent of it, only whites could own or occupy property, and in the other 10 percent the condition was reversed. The American ploy failed when the Supreme Court in *Buchanan v. Warley* (1917) voided a Louisville ordinance on the grounds that it limited the rights of property owners, not that it was discriminatory. Cities such as Atlanta continued to adopt variations on racial zoning for several years, testing the decision for loopholes, but eventually shifted to "race-neutral" zoning that discriminated instead by economic status.

South Africa's apartheid system drew on a long tradition of cities segregated by religion and ethnicity. Commercial cities in Eurasia often set aside sections where merchants from trading partners could live according to their own customs—Hindi quarters in cities of the central Asia silk route, Muslim quarters in Chinese cities, a section for Eastern Orthodox Greeks in Roman Catholic Venice. The early modern states of Europe established Jewish ghettos by law as well as custom (the term was first used in Venice in 1516). Two centuries later, the British East India Company divided Madras (Chennai) into a "white city" and a "black city." British authorities applied the system widely through their growing nineteenth-century empire, providing the model and training ground for white South Africans in the twentieth century.

If South Africa provided a failed model for American land use zoning, Germany provided a successful one. The first German planning law from 1875 authorized cities to set building standards and write master plans. Planning action accelerated in the 1890s in Berlin, Dusseldorf, Hamburg, and especially Frankfurt, which established land use zones with different sets of permitted activities and building regulations. In 1902 Frankfurt acquired the power to expropriate land for public purposes such as housing. Americans admired German city planners as scientific professionals. Influential commentators like Daniel Burnham and Benjamin Marsh, the key organizer for the first national conference on city planning in the United States, saw Frankfurt as an ideal model for the sorts of regulations they hoped to implement. Urban reformer Frederick C. Howe thought that Germany had the most wonderful cities of the new century.

New York usually gets the credit as the first American city to adopt comprehensive zoning, but it followed the model of Los Angeles as well as German examples. Los Angeles in 1908 delimited five residential districts where businesses were strictly limited and eight industrial districts, although they did not cover the entire city. Then, in 1916, New York approved its landmark zoning ordinance (muting the German connection because of World War I). The ordinance covered the entire city. It was both functional and physical, placing limits on how you could use a piece of land and what you could build on it. The law divided New York into residential, commercial, and unrestricted use zones and added five categories of height limitations, pushing New Yorkers to build the "step-pyramid" buildings that are common in much of Manhattan.

Zoning spread rapidly in North America. Twenty-four cities emulated New York within a year and roughly five hundred did so within a decade. The first schemes were simple. Chicago in 1923 divided itself into a single-family zone, an apartment zone, a commercial zone, and an industrial "anything goes" zone. The much smaller municipality of Point Grey, British Columbia (soon to merge with Vancouver), needed only three zones. The US Department of Commerce, under the leadership of Herbert Hoover, promoted a Standard State Zoning Enabling Act (1924) that states could adapt to authorize local zoning laws. By 1930 more than half the urban population of the United States lived in one of the eight hundred cities and towns with zoning. Although the tool started simple, the impulse to fine-tune has been inescapable. Twenty-first-century zoning is a complex of zones, subzones, and overlays for special design districts, historic districts, employment districts, and environmentally sensitive districts.

Zoning is properly a tool for implementing comprehensive plans. Comprehensive plans set the goals for a city's future, projecting population and economic growth, evaluating land needs, and allocating those needs among different parts of the city. Preparation is a visioning process that should involve a wide range of community groups and interests to develop a consensus about land use, housing needs, transportation needs, community facilities, economic development, and environmental protection. The process usually results in general goals, specific action items and targets, and a map of projected land patterns and facilities. The plan is both an optimistic vision and a to-do list that may include zoning changes.

Zoning has much to recommend it as a way to provide certainty within the real estate market, and it is deeply embedded as a city planning tool, but it also carries a class bias. The landmark legal case in the United States was *Village of Euclid v. Ambler Realty Company* (1926). The Supreme Court upheld the authority of a suburban Cleveland village to zone a portion of the land owned by the Ambler Company for single-family or two-family dwellings only, denying the company the right to develop its entire tract for commerce and industry. Was Euclid's ordinance a valid exercise of the police power or merely an exercise in "eccentric and supersensitive taste"? Previous decisions had validated legislation on building heights, construction standards, and lot coverage, and the court now concluded that there was no good basis on which to reject limitations on uses, even if they favored the affluent over the working class.

Euclid opened the door to exclusionary zoning, sometimes called "snob zoning," favored by affluent suburban cities in the name of "community character." A jurisdiction may simply fail to zone land for apartments. It may require very large lots for single-family houses, mandate minimum size for new houses, or include expensive design requirements such as a high ratio of bathrooms to bedrooms. Designation of older residential neighborhoods as historic districts may have an exclusionary impact by limiting adaptation of older houses and new infill construction. Parking requirements for apartment buildings also make the units more expensive and limit lower-income residents.

Class discrimination is automatically racial discrimination because of the racially unequal distribution of economic resources, including access to good jobs and financial capital from inheritance and real estate appreciation. Analysis of larger American metropolitan areas shows that jurisdictions with building permit caps or exclusively low-density zoning are less likely to have Hispanic and African American residents. Exclusionary zoning thus supplements or replaces other tools of racial discrimination. In the late 1930s, the US Home Owners Loan Corporation sponsored the creation of so-called redlining maps in which local officials and experts divided their cities into four color-coded districts from best (green) through still desirable (blue), declining (yellow), and hazardous (red!). The maps were intended to calibrate risk for mortgage lenders. They took into account not only housing conditions but also an assumed ranking of more and less desirable races and national origin groups. In the years since, "redlining" has come to mean neighborhood-level discrimination in mortgage lending and property insurance coverage, sometimes abetted by city plans that write off certain older neighborhoods as ripe for clearance or transition to nonresidential uses. Because of the obvious racism of the practice, the United States banned it with the Fair Housing Act of 1968, but informal rankings of neighborhoods remain alive among real estate investors.

The antidote to housing exclusion is inclusionary zoning. In the simplest form, inclusionary zoning requires that cities and towns zone at least some of their land for multifamily housing, although the provision does not guarantee apartments will be affordable. State courts moved New Jersey in this direction in deciding cases brought against the upscale community of Mt. Laurel. Similarly, the program created in response to the decision in *Gartreaux v. Chicago Housing Authority* (1969), which mandates the dispersal of low-income households throughout the region, has had some success in improving life chances for children. A big-city approach, available in some states but forbidden in others, is to require the builders of new apartments to include a certain percentage of units rented at below-market rates. This approach works best in hot real estate markets where developers or market-rate tenants are willing to absorb the transfer of costs.

A milder version of inclusive zoning is rezoning single-family districts to allow construction of "missing middle" housing such as duplexes, triplexes, row houses, and courtyard apartments. Accessory dwelling units or "mother-in-law apartments" can be added by converting basement or garage space into small apartments. Popular in the early twentieth century, this sort of moderate-density housing fell out of favor after World War II. Advocates argue that it can be built unobtrusively and will lower overall housing costs by increasing supply, with the secondary benefit of increasing residential density and supporting community services. Minneapolis in 2018 allowed duplexes and triplexes in all its single-family zones. California and Oregon in 2019 adopted state legislation that effectively overrides exclusive single-family zoning to allow auxiliary housing units and small multiunit structures.

The dynamics of inequality

Inclusive zoning and housing policies are important because the concentration of poor people, and especially the concentration of poor people of racial or ethnic minorities, creates a vicious cycle of disadvantage. Extreme poverty neighborhoods, defined as those with over 40 percent poor residents, have high percentages of single-parent households where adults may have erratic employment or juggle multiple low-paying jobs. There is little access to the informal networks through which workers find most jobs and few economically successful and stable householders as role models. An epidemic of evictions means that children have unstable school experiences and adults have difficulty forming and maintaining supportive social networks. When residents lack time, energy, and resources to spare from daily survival, it is no surprise that city bureaucracies find it easy to neglect poverty neighborhoods while responding to squeaky wheels in richer neighborhoods.

Poverty neighborhoods can follow several trajectories. They can fester interminably as zones of disadvantage, with anyone who is able to move being replaced by a low-income newcomer. In cities with declining populations—Rust Belt cities in Europe and North America, for example—such neighborhoods may be effectively abandoned, since no one is available to replace residents who move or die. Detroit and St. Louis offer stark American examples. The third possibility is disinvestment and devaluation of neighborhood property followed by a rising curve of reinvestment usually called gentrification—a term originally coined to describe the transformation of London neighborhoods. As rents rise, as subdivided houses are returned to single-family occupancy, and as new businesses outbid older businesses for commercial space, the result of gentrification is displacement of earlier residents by more affluent newcomers.

The investment involved in gentrification is part of the same cycling of capital that has remade city centers, although channeling through many small deals rather than a few megaprojects. The revitalized and upscaled neighborhoods serve the global economy as homes for knowledge workers who fill downtown offices. Prime candidates for gentrification are likely to have desirable locations close to the city center, amenities like parks or views, and older but interesting and "fixable" buildings. This might mean an industrial loft and warehouse area like SoHo in Manhattan or a close-in working-class neighborhood that was historically on the "wrong" side of the city like Hackney, Tower Hamlets, and Stratford in London.

The process starts with disinvestment in housing, often through landlord neglect, lagging maintenance of public infrastructure, and sometimes direct devaluation in formal plans. Real estate that is well located and extremely cheap then attracts "pioneers" who like the funky ambiance, commonly stereotyped as hippies, artists, and gay men. Incremental upgrades attract younger households and individual investors to fix up buildings, and their success in raising real estate values attracts corporate investors who tear down and replace old houses and low-rise commercial buildings with denser and more upscale development. When this sequence occurs in a sparsely populated warehouse or factory district near the urban core, it is urban revitalization. When it affects a poor but viable neighborhood, it means gentrification and displacement. In the global economy, residential investment can cross national boundaries, with Hong Kong and Taiwanese families buying second houses in Sydney and British buyers bidding up real estate in Lisbon.

City planners abet gentrification by defining areas as ripe for transformation. They can also try to mitigate it with programs to support "incumbent upgrading," helping neighborhood residents make their own improvements with housing grants and low-interest loans, neighborhood marketing, and support of local community development corporations that work on housing and economic development. The Lair Hill neighborhood in Portland, Oregon, is a remnant of an immigrant neighborhood on the edge of downtown that was largely cleared by Urban Renewal. In 1967 the Planning Bureau described the remaining fragment as "appropriate for clearance style urban renewal [with] few buildings which merit preservation or enhancement." A single decade later, the same agency called it "one of the finest collections of Victorian residential architecture" in the city, a change of heart that allowed it to retain a funky hippie ambiance for another generation. Neighborhood conservation efforts are particularly important for neighborhoods with strong ethnic identities, since they are likely to house key institutions such as churches, social clubs, weekly newspapers, and civic organizations that foster group identity.

In North America, a consequence of gentrification and displacement has been to challenge the long-established class gradient in which housing values and social status increase with distance from the city center—the classic model of concentric rings that sociologists at the University of Chicago defined in the 1910s and 1920s. In prosperous cities with strong white-collar economies, better educated and affluent households have been remaking—gentrifying—inner neighborhoods, pushing racial minorities and working-class folks into the older suburban ring. Rates of poverty have been growing more rapidly in suburbs than in central cities for several decades, and more rapidly than overall suburban population growth, and American suburbs now have more poor people than do central cities.

The fast-growing presence of immigrants in North American suburbs is related, since suburbs can provide affordable housing that is easy to move into. Old ethnic neighborhoods have faded, and places like Scarborough on the east side of Toronto are centers of ethnic life. Many suburban school districts have more ethnic and racial variety than central city schools. Older suburbs offer affordable space for immigrant entrepreneurship and the natural revitalization of well-worn commercial strips, making the Asian mall a common feature of North American cityscapes. Similarly, immigrants from Latin America have brought new life to older city neighborhoods in the United States. They reuse old commercial strips and turn front yards and sidewalks into sites for sociability, producing many of the goals of New Urbanism without theoretical fuss and bother.

However, migration can also bring cultural values about urban living into conflict even as professional planning shares common standards and expectations across international borders. Planning issues arise over cultural differences in the use of public spaces like parks and streets and over housing choices that may violate previous local norms. A notorious nonsuburban example is the resistance in 1990s Vancouver to "monster houses," large, blocky houses intended for multiple generations that Chinese immigrants built in established upscale neighborhoods. Despite the consternation of some Anglo-Canadian residents, the big houses have remained to add ethnic and architectural variety to quiet, leafy streets.

Alternative voices

In 1967, members of the American Institute of Planners (AIP, a predecessor of the American Planning Association) argued vehemently over the definition of planning. Since 1938, the AIP constitution had defined the field as "the planning of the unified development of urban communities and their environs and of states, regions and the nation, as expressed through determination of the comprehensive arrangement of land uses and land occupancy and the regulation thereof." Now, after emotional debates, the AIP dropped the final phrase and added social and economic planning to its definition.

Both the public and practitioners had tended to view the design professions as primary, and their approach had dominated city-planning education in the first decades of the twentieth century. Architects like Le Corbusier and Frank Lloyd Wright dominated public discussion of urban futures. In the 1950s, transportation planners who began to work with large data sets reinvigorated the engineering–planning nexus that had contributed to the field's origins in the previous century. At the same time, however, planners were turning toward the social sciences and urban studies. The key document was Harvey Perloff's 1957 book *The Education of City Planners*. Perloff was then the head of the planning program at the University of Chicago, the center of systematic research on urban society. He called for a planning curriculum that emphasized systematic knowledge of cities as functioning systems that are shaped by and shape social and technological trends. He believed that planners needed to understand basic principles of socioeconomic change, develop hypotheses, and test these ideas with research. In short, planning educators should aim to train applied social scientists first, designers second.

The changing political dynamics of the 1960s and 1970s brought new emphasis on citizen and community input into planning decisions. The Community Action program (1965) and the Model Cities program (1967) of President Lyndon Johnson's War on Poverty required citizen consultation and participation in neighborhood planning decisions. The Community Development Block Grant program, begun in 1974, extended the participatory mandate. The result is a constant tension, sometimes creative and sometimes paralyzing, between community activists and professionally trained planners and consultants assigned to work on community plans. Sherry Arnstein, a policy specialist with the US Department of Housing and Urban Development, in 1969 described a "ladder of citizen participation" that recognizes the frequent gap between pro forma citizen consultation and substantial citizen influence on planning decisions. The ladder arrays participation approaches from manipulation and therapy through consultation and partnership to delegation and citizen control.

When the AIP changed its mission statement, the profession was absorbing activist planner Paul Davidoff's influential argument for "advocacy planning." Davidoff recognized that American planning had originated and developed with the support of local civic leaders and with a business-oriented agenda of facilitating efficient metropolitan growth. He also recognized that unequal access to expertise and information is a basic source of unequal power. He argued forcefully that planners should engage more directly in the struggle for equal civil and economic rights by using their expertise to work on behalf of disadvantaged segments of society. They should fight for their own progressive values and advocate for their clients' views of community betterment.

Equity planning is an important extension of Davidoff's ideas. The term was notably applied in Cleveland in the 1970s. A city planning staff led by Norman Krumholz tried to keep the needs and concerns of the city's poorest neighborhoods and citizens on the public agenda. The practice requires support in city hall (provided by Carl Stokes and Dennis Kucinich in Cleveland, for example) as well as enough political savvy on the part of planners to develop equity-based projects that remain acceptable for the city as a whole. Equity planning is thus a pragmatic and politically savvy effort to build alliances with neighborhood activists and find ways to persuade business interests and the middle class that helping poor communities benefits the entire city. Mayor Harold Washington applied the lessons of Cleveland to Chicago, whose economic development plan of 1984 was explicitly intended to redistribute the benefits of economic growth more equitably among groups and neighborhoods. Underlying this planning approach is the work of French sociologist Henri Lefebvre, who wrote about "the right to the city," the idea that every resident should have full access to the benefits and pleasures of their urban community through empowerment planning, political participation, and radical activism if necessary.

Through all of this work, planners have faced a tension between working within existing institutions and power structures and seeking to assist the emergence of new social and political movements that may challenge those institutions. A variation that leans toward the latter is empowerment planning, which emphasizes the importance of grassroots action. In this model, community voices are primary and planners are facilitators who work closely with community residents to help the community itself define its problems and solutions. Local knowledge that is held and articulated by residents themselves balances professional expertise. Although plans and projects are important goals, the process itself, and the capacities that it develops among its participants, is equally important. Empowerment planning thus reaches back in its intellectual framework to the Community Action and Model Cities programs of the 1960s and finds expression in grassroots community development work.

Community organizing helped to add women's voices and concerns to a profession and practice that had been overwhelmingly the province of white males. Women played a prominent role in the definition of urban problems in the early twentieth century, such as the researchers and activists associated with Hull House in Chicago. In the 1920s and 1930s, however, male practitioners increasingly defined planning in terms of physical design and legal regulations. The social concerns of early women reformers either spun off into the emerging field of social work or were isolated within the narrower silo of housing reform, where individuals such as Americans Catherine Bauer Wurster and Edith Elmer Wood, both advocates of affordable housing as writers, organizers, and consultants, had substantial influence on federal housing policy. To the surprise of nobody who understands the midcentury gender divide in the professions, women like Britain's Jacqueline Tyrwhitt, whose interests focused on urban design, did their work in the shadow of more prominent men. At the same time, women working in midlevel roles in planning, design, and real estate played essential roles in implementing the plans and schemes of the prominent men who dominated the press releases.

Women who mobilized around neighborhood issues or joined in the new structures for citizen participation played by their own rules. They lacked the time to attend bureaucratic planning commission meetings at City Hall, but they could come out in force when planners, usually the new hires, ventured to their school gyms, church basements, and community centers. Their agendas focused on the problems of everyday life—streets that were good for cars but bad for children, rundown and unsafe parks, and poor schools. They often organized to confront the establishment, calling out both racism and class bias. Their work did not look like the planning taught in graduate schools, but women like Beatrice Gallegos with Communities United for Public Service in San Antonio or Lois Gibbs, who forced the cleanup of the Love Canal chemical dump in Buffalo, powerfully reshaped urban landscapes.

The planning profession itself has also changed. Researchers and students in the 1980s and 1990s called attention to the neglect of women's concerns in land use planning and design. They have called for designers to make parks, bus stops, and other public spaces safer for women. They have modified land use regulations that use very narrow definitions of "family." They argue for more flexible public transportation options. They challenge land use planners to recognize that women tend to make more daily trips than men when commuting, shopping, and transporting children are considered together, creating support for mixed-use development and twenty-minute neighborhoods, where essential services are dispersed through the city. These are common issues that can unite women across class differences.

The Australian Canadian planning theorist and filmmaker Leonie Sandercock has promoted empowerment planning as a tool for creating inclusive cities. She argues that comprehensive, top-down, and expert-driven planning neglects too much of everyday experience. Any freshly hired planner with a new graduate degree who is sent from city hall to work with a low-income or minority neighborhood soon learns that citizens have long memories about failed plans from decades before. They understand their community by telling stories about how it has grown, changed, and been helped or damaged by city efforts. Transformative planning requires participants to respect multiple frameworks of understanding and multiple forms of expression, including expressions of anger and hurt.

Sandercock frames her arguments with the deliberately uneasy metaphor of "mongrel cities," meaning cities of multicultural richness and cross-fertilization. The urban condition in the twenty-first century is one in which "difference, otherness, fragmentation, splintering, multiplicity, heterogeneity, [and] plurality prevail." The challenge is to realize "the possibility of living alongside others who are different, learning from them, creating new worlds with them, instead of fearing them." Although from a very different ideological position, Sandercock's arguments would have resonated with John Stuart Mill, who wrote in 1848, "it is hardly possible to overrate the value, in the present low state of human development, of placing human beings in contact with persons dissimilar to themselves, and with modes of thought and action unlike those with which they are familiar. Such communication has always been one of the primary sources of progress."

Chapter 5
Metropolis and megaregion

Daniel Burnham's 1909 Plan of Chicago is filled with stunning images of potential cityscapes. The jewel-box depictions of civic temples and awesome public squares by artist Jules Guerin likened future Chicago to an imaginary Byzantium. They are one of the reasons why the plan is sometimes characterized as "city beautiful" planning. Nevertheless, what is most striking is the practicality and prescience of its regional scope.

The Plan of Chicago focused on transportation and the effective specialization of land uses for the greater Chicago area. It tried to frame the real estate market and the work of private city builders within a regional infrastructure of rationalized railroads and new highways. It knit downtown and surrounding neighborhoods, city to suburbs and surroundings to a distance of sixty miles. It transformed Chicago's booster vision of the nineteenth century into specific ideas for shaping a vast but functional cityscape. Economically comprehensive as well as spatially unifying, the plan envisioned a Chicago that located its different activities in their most efficient places. The heritage of the Plan of Chicago extends beyond northern Illinois. Burnham's collaborator Edward Bennett during the 1910s authored city-region plans for Detroit, Minneapolis, Portland, and Ottawa. These were comprehensive in topical coverage, advanced in technique, and spacious in their regional coverage.

His 1915 plan for Ottawa is typical. It dealt with railroads, traffic, streets, and regional parks. It too came with beautiful, distracting watercolor renderings, but the report contained the components of a comprehensive plan as would be suggested by American John Nolen in *City Planning* (1916) and British expert Thomas Adams in *Outline of Town and City Planning* (1935). Bennett defined the underlying issue as coping with economic growth: "Growth, expansion, is the most potent factor in this study. Wherever there is growth there are powerful forces at work, needing only to be directed to produce fine results, the linking together and relating of various sections of a city plan.... Commerce and economy must underlie this study."

These comprehensive plans appeared when Americans were thinking through the implications of horizontal growth and the

6. Edward Bennett's 1915 plan for the Canadian capital region of Ottawa and Hull envisioned a monumental center for Ottawa City. Beautiful plans for places like Washington and Chicago featured meticulously drawn maps and inspiring perspective drawings modeled on the newly rebuilt capitals of Europe.

emergence of large urbanized regions. New York had consolidated five counties into a single supercity in 1898, and Chicago had recently tripled its area through annexations. Berlin would do likewise in 1920 to become the third-largest city in the industrial world. At the same historical moment, the US Census Bureau was figuring out how to measure newly sprawling urban regions, coining the term "metropolitan district" in 1910. Chicago, of course, was number two, with 2,456,000 metropolitan residents, putting it behind New York but comfortably ahead of Philadelphia.

The challenge for metropolitan-regional planning remains the same as Burnham and Bennett faced a century ago—to find ways to "control" and channel fast-growing populations and expanding economic activities in ways that increase efficiency and maintain metro areas as integrated, functional wholes. In 1909, the fast-growing industrial cities like Berlin, Milan, and Pittsburgh exemplified the scale and pace of urban growth. More recently, new-economy cities like Bangalore, Shenzhen, and Seattle have been the frontiers of urban change.

Major metropolitan regions are challenged to develop growth plans that reenact the fundamental goals of the Plan of Chicago and at similar geographic scale. The Puget Sound Regional Council has written successive Vision 2020, Vision 2040, and Vision 2050 plans for a multicentered Tacoma–Seattle–Everett region. The Greater Sydney Commission has envisioned a "Metropolis of Three Cities" reaching from beaches to the Blue Mountains. These plans address their metropolitan regions on a Burnham/Bennett scale. They emphasize the integration of centers and suburbs through a system of nodes and arteries, look for ways to build in open space, and recognize the need to allocate space for the production segments of the economy.

The organization of regional planning

Efforts at regional planning respond to governmental complexity as well as increasing size. At the center of nearly every urban area is a city or municipality that is a bounded governmental unit with an identifiable name: Sapporo, Winnipeg, Hamburg. The core municipality itself may be small like Adelaide (population twenty thousand) or large like Paris (two million). Surrounding that core city are other municipalities—dozens or even hundreds in a case like Los Angeles or Chicago—that extend the developed urban area. National statistical agencies often recognize this functional region with terms such as "urban area" (United States), "built-up area" (United Kingdom), or *unité urbaine* (France). To add complication, several nations (India, Argentina, Brazil, France, Canada, the United States) delimit larger metropolitan areas that encompass the urban area plus additional territory that is less heavily developed but closely connected to the urban core by commuting and other economic ties. Local residents know the subdivisions but outsiders do not, so someone might say "I'm from Howick" when talking locally with someone else from the Auckland area, but "I'm from Auckland" when brashly striking up a conversation in a waiting area at LAX or Changi airport.

The terminology of urban areas and metropolitan areas is descriptive, an attempt to get a handle on the complex and constantly changing geography of big cities and their environs. Metropolitan area data are beloved of economic development planners and the owners of professional sports teams because the metropolis is essentially a daily and weekly market area—both a labor market and a consumer market. Bigger is usually better in the economic development field, so imprecise terms like the Dallas Metroplex or Greater Bristol (United Kingdom) abound. In 2017, when Amazon solicited proposals from American cities that wanted to be chosen for a second headquarters, the first stated preference was for "metropolitan areas with a population of one million or more."

The economic development departments or private business organizations that responded to Amazon could largely ignore the contradictions inherent in the division of metropolitan regions among multiple governments. Practical planners cannot, because planning is done within and by the authority of governmental entities. It has long been glaringly obvious that political and administrative boundaries are hard put to keep up with the dynamics of urban growth. Political units develop vested interests, constituencies, and bureaucracies that are often resistant to solutions that transcend their boundaries or require allocation of costs and benefits across a metropolitan region. Poor people have to live somewhere, but most component municipalities would prefer more upscale housing and would rather avoid public or social housing. As a result, experiments with "fair share" allocation of affordable housing, as in the Dayton, Ohio, region in the 1970s, usually have limited success. Similarly, nearly all residents of the metro region would like a modern and convenient airport, but most would prefer it be located at just enough distance that planes take off and land over someone else's neighborhood.

The easiest option for dealing with regional problems is to create single-issue agencies to plan and deliver physical services such as public transit, air pollution abatement, airports and maritime shipping terminals, and water supply. The agency may be created cooperatively by participating local governments or established by a higher level of government such as an Australian state. The common result is to find services planned and managed in multiple tiers—a regional parks board plus park and recreation departments in individual cities and towns, each controlling and managing distinct parcels of land. Streets and roads are a particular muddle in American cities. Regional planners set area priorities through consultation and compromise among governments as well as through technical analysis. State highway departments maintain freeways and develop expansion plans. Municipalities care for local streets and balance the expectations of automobile users with bicycle riders (remove auto traffic lanes for bike lanes?) and transit agencies (create dedicated busways in the street right of way?). Transit agencies independently plan rail lines that also compete for street space.

A further step is a formal two-tier system in which a metropolitan-scale government exercises multiple powers. In North America, Toronto was the model to be emulated. The province of Ontario in 1954 created the Municipality of Metropolitan Toronto as a second tier of government embracing the central city and surrounding communities. Responsible for major regional issues such as public transportation, arterial roads, water and sewer facilities, and regional parks, it functioned until 1998, when the province—over local opposition—created a single City of Toronto covering the same broad area. Two thousand kilometers to the west, Manitoba's provincial government in 1960 created a Metropolitan Corporation of Greater Winnipeg with an elected council to serve as a second tier of government dealing with regional issues while the old city and suburbs handled local concerns. Twelve years later, the leftist New Democratic Party created a single Unicity, gaining uniform services and tax rate with a government where suburban votes could dominate.

New Zealand in 2010 created a single Auckland Council as a supercity that consolidated several previously separate municipalities, although with some functions devolved to twenty-one local boards. Portland, Oregon's, Metro is the only elected regional government in the United States, with council districts deliberately drawn to cut across city and county boundaries; it oversees regional planning, garbage disposal, regional parks, and major cultural venues and has become embedded in the political landscape after four decades.

Despite scattered success stories, regional governments and agencies often have weak and tenuous lives. They may have inadequate powers and political support, like the Commission for the Buenos Aires Metropolitan Area. They may be imposed by a central government on reluctant localities that think they are better able to negotiate regional solutions among themselves, as with the Metropole du Grand Paris, created in 2016 as a transportation planning organization covering seven million people in Paris and three adjacent *départements*. Leaders and residents of more progressive or leftist central cities sometimes see the creation of more spatially inclusive entities as a ploy to dilute their political influence and to increase that of more conservative suburbs. That was the concern in Paris, the reality in Toronto, and the story in London, where Margaret Thatcher's Conservative government abolished the London County Council (1965–86) for political and ideological reasons and where Tony Blair's Labour government reversed the action by creating a similar Greater London Authority in 1990.

Urban containment and growth management

The influence of Ebenezer Howard extends not only to the postwar popularity of New Towns but also to strategies for containing the outward expansion of urban development. England was early in implementing a comprehensive policy, passing the Greenbelt Corridor and Home Counties Act in 1938. It designated a very large ring of nonurban land around London as a rural zone to be protected from intensive development. The Greater London Plan of 1944 further institutionalized the London greenbelt, whose 1.2 million acres have remained substantially rural. Additional greenbelts have successfully restricted sprawl around eighteen other British cities and have kept towns separated by open space. Greenbelts have become an environmental as well as planning cause, and communities "outside" can see them as important tools for maintaining themselves as attractive middle-class exurbs and enclaves.

British Columbia in 1973 created an Agricultural Land Reserve that put the most productive farmland in the Fraser Valley, a clearly finite resource in the mountainous province, off limits for suburbanization. Hawaii set the pace in the United States with a 1966 law to protect the pineapple and sugar industries by dividing the state into urban, rural, agricultural, and conservation areas (somewhat like the British Columbia program). Oregon has taken the strongest steps in the United States, adopting a statewide land use planning system in 1973 to fend off what Governor Tom McCall called "the unfettered despoiling of the land" through "sagebrush subdivisions, coastal condomania, and the ravenous rampage of suburbia in the Willamette Valley." A key tool is the establishment of an Urban Growth Boundary (UGB) around every city and metropolitan area to protect productive farm and forest land and keep urban areas compact. Development outside the UGB must be related to farm and forest uses or meet stringent standards of need. However, UGBs are "skins" rather than "walls," expanding incrementally as cities grow and absorb available vacant land inside the boundary.

Oslo is another growth boundary city. Sited at the head of the long Oslofjord, it has adopted the slogan "the blue and the green and the city in between." Two-thirds of the area within the municipal boundary is *marka* (forest), whose lakes and trails are heavily used for recreation. The forest edge is as little as fifteen minutes from the city center. Development is prohibited beyond a *markagrensa* (forest boundary). Access to the outdoors is a deeply held value among Norwegians and the development boundary has enjoyed solid political support.

The Netherlands maintains an inside-out growth boundary. The nation's major cities of Amsterdam, Utrecht, Rotterdam, and The Hague and smaller connecting cities form a roughly circular *Randstad* or Ring City. The agricultural land in the middle of the ring is called the Green Heart, and the Green Heart/City Ring concept has been central to Dutch spatial planning since the 1950s. Land use regulations protect both farming and recreational space within the Green Heart to prevent suburban encroachment and the dreaded "Los Angeles syndrome." New development is

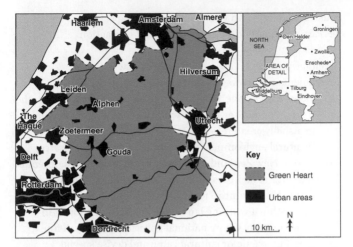

7. The Green Heart of the Netherlands is one of the success stories of regional planning. As a reverse greenbelt, it has effectively preserved open space and farmland within a ring of large Dutch cities.

instead directed toward connecting cities within along the circle: "Not outside the ring, not inside the ring into the Green Heart, but intensifying urban areas on the ring," according to a national policy statement.

Urban containment and farmland protection policies in Europe and North America developed within the progressive and regulatory policy orientation of the mid-twentieth century. The turn toward market solutions and free market ideology has raised criticisms, especially the argument that growth boundaries increase housing costs. Market advocates argue that restricting the supply of land drives up the total cost of new construction and inflates the price of existing housing. The counterargument, at least in North America, is that new housing should not require large suburban lots and that housing demand can be met with single-family housing on smaller lots and by opening zoning to allow the "missing middle" of duplex and triplex housing, row housing, and one- and two-story courtyard apartments, which increase neighborhood density and social interaction.

Greenline parks are a special instance of how national governments can manage sensitive landscapes where metropolitan uses penetrate into rural land. National parks in the United States and other nations with large areas of undeveloped land are usually created to preserve and protect spectacular or unique natural environments—Yosemite in the United States, Fiordland in New Zealand, Itatiaia in Brazil. New development is limited to tourist facilities, and private inholdings will likely be bought out. An alternative for preserving natural systems and amenities within a working landscape has been developed in Britain and Europe, where national governments may define a district of high scenic or cultural value and devise special land-management regulations to sustain its character over time. Inside the "green line" special controls can preserve natural resources and historic landscapes while allowing residents to continue their previous livelihoods from land-based industries. National parks in the United Kingdom are specially regulated landscapes rather than public reserves. Examples of this approach in the United States include the Adirondacks Park in New York, Pinelands National Reserve in New Jersey, and the Columbia River Gorge National Scenic Area in Washington and Oregon.

Megaregions and superregional development planning

Cities not only interact with contiguous territories to create individual city-regions. They also create even larger spatial patterns of both similarity and connection—somewhat like the way individual solar systems group into galaxies and galaxies into even vaster galactic clusters. Indeed, night satellite photos of the world, with thick ribbons of urban lights on some parts of the landscape and individual bright spots on others, make for an inescapable galactic analogy with isolated stars interspersed among glowing nebulae.

One way to explore these large patterns is to look for city-regions where formerly independent cities grow into each other to form something larger. The Scottish polymath Patrick Geddes introduced the term "conurbation" in 1915 to describe a region where large independent cities had effectively merged into each other, as with the Rhine-Ruhr district in Germany and the Randstad of the Netherlands. In the United States, this idea took root as Combined Statistical Areas, which link adjacent metropolitan regions such as Boston–Providence–Worcester and Washington–Baltimore for census statistics.

Some nations, such as Germany and the United States, have balanced urban systems in which several important metropolitan centers are competitive with each other, such as Hamburg, Munich, Frankfurt, Berlin, Stuttgart, Dusseldorf, and Cologne in the German case. Other nations have a single dominant city that is far larger and more economically powerful than any others, and national development and investment policy often tries to build up "growth poles" as counterweights. In the 1950s and 1960s, French planners and policy makers tried to convince their fellow citizens that Paris was sucking the life out of the rest of France and that Bordeaux and Lyon were perfectly acceptable alternatives. A key book was titled *Paris and the French Desert*. Ciudad Guayana was intended to counterbalance the influence of Caracas. New capital cities that are *not* Lagos, Jakarta, or Karachi are alternatives to those dominant cities. China's creation of Special Economic Zones is a variation. Shenzen is the first and most spectacular result, growing from a set of villages and small towns to a megacity of twenty million in forty years.

Place three or four conurbations end to end and the result is a megalopolis. The French geographer Jean Gottmann introduced the term in 1961 when he identified the entire Boston–Washington

81

corridor as an interconnected urban complex where individual cities retained their identities but also networked as a larger region four hundred miles in length. Gottmann recognized that abundant farmland and open space intervened among the several cities and their suburbs, but he also argued that the intensities of interaction by road, rail, and telephone linked these cities into a distinct super metropolitan entity. The Greek planner Constantinos Doxiadis applied the same sort of thinking to Detroit and the Great Lakes region (on his way to coming up with the idea of a globe-spanning ecumenopolis). Journalists and academics soon caught the megalopolis bug. The US Census Bureau rule of defining metropolitan areas by county boundaries makes it easy to eyeball a map and see two or three distinct metro areas reaching out to embrace each other. Especially in the 1960s and 1970s it was a bit of a parlor game in the United States to identify BosWash rivals with names like ChiPitts around the Great Lakes and SanSan in California.

Gottmann's concept and even terminology migrated easily to other settings. Japan's Taiheiyō Belt (Pacific Belt) from Tokyo to Osaka and beyond is sometimes termed "megaroporisu." Seeking an objective basis for transnational economic strategies in the European Union, planners there have explored the ways in which sets of metropolitan areas string together in spatial units that are even larger than Megalopolis and that sometimes get cute names: the Blue Banana that curves from Manchester to Milan through the historic heartland of economic Europe and the Golden Banana along the Mediterranean coast from Valencia to Genoa. In Asia a common term is "mega-urban region".

The challenge in this grand spatial thinking is to identify a realistic scale for the robust economic interactions expected in an era of increasing global connectivity. Multi city regions can include long recognized conurbations like the English Midlands, rapidly urbanizing areas like China's Pearl River Delta, and binational regions such as Copenhagen–Malmo. In contrast, the imaginative Copenhagen–Stockholm–Helsinki–St. Petersburg constellation seems more like a cruise ship itinerary than a functional region.

In turn, this highly evolved spatial thinking reentered the twenty-first-century United States as megaregions. According to its proponents, a megaregion is a large, connected network of metropolitan areas that share enough economic and cultural similarities to be useful units for making policy decisions. They are also seen as components of the global economy that are more natural and dynamic than states (see references for a link to megaregion maps). The New York–oriented Regional Plan Association and think tanks such as the Lincoln Institute of Land Policy have promoted and developed the concept, and evolving ideas have been repeatedly published in planning magazines, essay collections, and a variety of web-based documents. The current North American versions of megaregions include some with clear historic and current identities, such as the venerable Boston–Washington corridor. The Great Lakes industrial region includes the Canadian industrial heartland in Ontario. Southern California inevitably includes Tijuana and northern Baja California.

China has been doing urban development on an especially grand scale. The Pearl River Delta, with sixty million people in nine mainland cities plus Hong Kong and Macau, is perhaps the biggest megacity of all. It also demonstrates the challenges to planning on such a large scale. The Chinese government's Pearl River Delta Greater Bay Area Integration Plan is a massive transportation investment program of highways, rail lines, and a $13 billion bridge connecting Hong Kong, Zhuhai, and Macau. The goal is to help the region transition from lower-value export manufacturing to innovative and high-tech manufacturing, while the individual cities remain competitive among themselves.

Planning at this scale has a large element of wishful thinking mixed in with the practical. As in southeastern China, it tends to focus on aspirations around economic development and commonly zeroes in on large-scale transportation investments to better integrate the different cities and subregions. Nevertheless, city planning remains overwhelmingly a local and regional, not superregional, activity. Visionaries can dream about an ecumenopolis, but city planning as a profession is just a century old. Practicing planners continue to focus on community livability and land use changes, continue to draw authority from local and regional levels of government, and continue to establish legitimacy in the eyes of the public by how their work improves everyday life.

Chapter 6
Nature in the city

Coyotes are common in Native American stories as tricksters and sometimes helpers to humankind. They are also indelibly fixed in the imagination of an American generation as creatures of the desert Southwest through dozens of cartoons pitting Wile E. Coyote against Road Runner. The coyote of Looney Tunes and the coyote of Arikara or Navaho legends are unquestionably rural, but twenty-first-century coyotes do more than howl from mesa tops. They hang out in Central Park and on the Columbia University campus. Several thousand live in Chicago and its suburbs, and thousands more roam the hills and ravines where Los Angeles fingers its way into surrounding mountains. Stream beds, railroad lines, parks, golf courses, campuses, and vacant lots provide urban access and living space for coyotes and other mammals—wild boars in Genoa, deer at pest levels in the northeastern United States. Coyotes occasionally saunter down the middle of the street in front of my house three miles from the center of Portland, Oregon.

Coyotes and other urban animals are reminders that cities are natural environments. They may be vast artifacts whose sculpted forms of brick, wood, steel, and concrete serve human needs, but they are embedded in natural settings and enmeshed in natural systems. They support songbirds, rats, bees, shade trees, and weeds. We plan for the natural city by designing open space into the urban fabric, managing its metabolism, and trying to reduce energy use and greenhouse gas emissions. A major goal in city planning is to preserve and reintroduce natural landscapes and systems within the built environment, whether through traditional options such as parks or innovative techniques to deal with storm water and cleanse air. The efficient management of interactions between the natural city and the built city is essential to its survival and connects directly to the health of its residents.

Parks and open space

Back Bay is a classic and elegant Boston neighborhood, built in the later nineteenth century on filled tidal wetlands where the Charles River entered Boston Harbor. Stately townhouses line broad Parisian-style avenues that extend westward from the Public Garden. The west end of Back Bay meets the Fens, a meandering park and watercourse that landscape architect Frederick Law Olmsted sculpted from an unfilled section of the same marshland. It is now part of Boston's Emerald Necklace of interconnected parks and parkways. The contrast between the two landscapes encapsulates a basic choice in city planning—the common choice to manipulate the natural landscape for building sites and the alternative of preserving open space as parks and natural areas within the built fabric of the city.

Olmsted was a seminal figure in city planning. Earlier parks in European cities had commonly been designed for the elite, laid out in formal design, such as the Jardin du Luxembourg in Paris, and sometimes derived from royal precincts. Olmsted offered both a design alternative, emphasizing natural vegetation and forms, and an ideology of parks. Fully realized parks renewed cities physically and have often been described as "the lungs of the city" for the very real capacity of trees and greenery to filter air pollution. They had the social function of recreation for both upper-class and working people. Olmsted also saw large parks as places of refuge and spiritual renewal, designing them to bring a sense of natural landscape into the city.

Olmsted's pioneering project was Central Park in New York. Partnering with a more experienced park designer, the English-born Calvert Vaux, he entered and won a design competition for a large new open space on the northern edge of the developed city. Implementation began in 1858. With its sunken roads, limited formal elements, open spaces, and tracts of unmanicured vegetation, the park was intended to allow visitors to escape from the intensity of the city for relatively passive and individualized experiences.

Paris mirrored Central Park with the Parc des Buttes-Chaumont and dwarfed it with the Bois de Boulogne. Established by Baron Georges Haussmann as part of his massive modernization of Paris, designed by Jean-Claude Alphand, and opened in 1867, the Parc des Buttes-Chaumont transformed abandoned quarries and a barren hillside on the eastern edge of the city into a mix of formal and natural areas that retain their attraction 150 years later. The Bois de Boulogne combined formal and naturalized sections to satisfy the desire of Napoleon III for a Parisian counterpart to London's Hyde Park. In North America, Olmsted and his coworkers developed and elaborated the model of the large immersive park with Montreal's Mount Royal Park, Detroit's Belle Isle Park, and Brooklyn's Prospect Park, which he considered his best work. Shunning symmetrical elements, he used long curving meadows, irregular lakes, and winding pathways to create a feeling of country in the city. Olmsted also strove to place individual parks as parts of a larger system. He and his firm were involved with such sites as the Jackson Park–Washington Park complex in Chicago, the park system for Buffalo, New York, and the Louisville, Kentucky, parkway system.

With Olmsted as its most visible proponent, park development introduced Americans to systematic planning at a regional scale.

He was part of a larger national movement for urban parks in which other landscape designers pursued similar goals. H. W. S. Cleveland, author of *Landscape Design as Applied to the Wants of the West* (1873), designed a comprehensive system for Minneapolis and St. Paul in the 1880s. George Kessler did the same for Kansas City in the 1890s. The regional park system for greater Boston, planned by a Metropolitan Park Commission established in 1893, expanded on Olmsted's plans and by 1902 embraced fifteen thousand acres, ten miles of shoreline, and twenty-two miles of parkway. Regional park systems of the early twentieth century, such as the Cook County Forest Preserves outside Chicago and Denver Mountain Parks, extended regional open space planning into the automobile age. These plans required that civic leaders think about population growth, land uses, and circulation on a regional scale and acquire land in advance of need, often turning environmentally sensitive areas that are difficult to build on, such as steep hills, marshes, lakefronts, and stream courses, into parks and parkways.

Metropolitan areas continue to acquire and protect undeveloped land on the urban fringe in anticipation of population growth, often through regional parks or service agencies. Individual municipalities maintain large older parks with a mix of passive and active recreation and sometimes tensions between the preferences of different classes and ethnic groups—walkers versus mountain bikers, softball diamonds and soccer pitches versus flower displays, open meadows versus restaurants (in the nineteenth century it was genteel strollers versus beer gardens). They also manage smaller neighborhood parks and playgrounds for children's and youth sports.

Park and open space planning raises equity questions. Should available funds be allocated to acquire more open space and natural areas on the urban fringe before it is too late, expanding open space available to more affluent residents with personal automobiles? Is the money better used to develop and improve neighborhood parks in poorer inner-city neighborhoods with less mobile populations? Do parks in those lower-income areas get as much attention as those in affluent neighborhoods where residents know how to lobby local officials? Do parks invite socially inclusive or exclusive use? The Los Angeles suburb of Lakewood, "Tomorrow's City Today," grew after World War II around dozens of parks and playgrounds that helped to parcel the development into distinct communities. Residents of each neighborhood staked a claim to "their" park, and kids ventured into other parks only at the invitation of a friend. When Latino and African American residents began to replace original white families in the 1990s, shared use of the same parks was a point of tension. The problem, according to former Lakewood resident Alida Brill, was that Lakewood had developed "the feeling of a club—the feeling that because everyone started out together, residents are entitled to lifetime 'charter membership.'"

Stoking the urban metabolism: energy and water

Like a living creature, a city has a metabolism. It takes in energy and resources, converts some into the urban fabric, and produces waste residues. Some of the inputs require no human intervention—the air that moves with the wind, water that moves with the tides. Other resources are deliberately imported. Cities reach into the countryside for wood, gravel, sand, and other building materials, for natural gas, and for electricity. They import inputs for their factories, consumer goods, and food. Water flows through kitchen faucets, fire hydrants, and factory valves because feats of engineering are matched with creative institutional arrangements. Some of the imports remain in the city to sustain human life or end up in buildings and pavements, but others change form into waste. Cities generate excess heat, cast particulates and chemicals into the sky, wash lawn fertilizer and street residues into streams, and ship garbage and rubble to landfills that may be hundreds of miles distant. In this fundamental way, cities have to be planned as components within a larger natural world.

Cities depend on three large-scale and comprehensive infrastructure systems. Transportation facilities are the most evident. Residents walk on sidewalks, pedal along bikeways, drive on streets and freeways, ride trams and subways, text car services, dodge delivery vans, and fly out of airports. If they know where to look, they can view railroad freight yards and, in port cities, the massive cranes of container terminals.

Energy infrastructure is less visible. A century ago, piles of coal were carted to individual houses, factories, and gasification plants. Now most urban energy arrives from a distance via high-voltage wires and gas pipelines. Ice and wind storms remind us about the fragility of electric wires and occasional explosions remind us about gas lines, but we usually turn on lights and dial up thermostats without thinking infrastructure thoughts.

The third massive infrastructure system moves water. One set of pipes carries water from distant sources to individual taps. Another set drains rainwater from streets. A third collects used water from households and businesses for treatment and return to nearby rivers and lakes. Sewers have a high yuck factor but they also figure in the imagination as a hidden, underground city. Victor Hugo in *Les Miserables* sent Jean Valjean though the Paris sewers newly built by George Haussmann as the complement to his elegant boulevards. Contemporary Teenage Mutant Ninja Turtles happily hang out and eat pizza in the sewers of a cartoon New York.

Energy and water link vast hinterlands to the everyday lives of city people as cities reach further and further for the resources that help them grow. The first "long-distance" transmission of hydroelectric power in the United States was fourteen miles into Portland, Oregon, in 1889. Within half a century, Grand Coulee

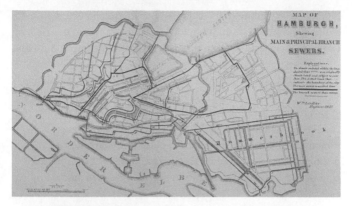

8. **Nineteenth-century cities invested as much effort and money in modern sewer systems as they did on new streets. Experts and expertise circulated widely among European and American cities. In Hamburg, Germany, a new sewer system was designed by an English expert, William Lindley, who would also work in Warsaw and Budapest, and it provided a model for Chicago.**

Dam was sending electricity hundreds of miles to Portland and Seattle and Boulder Dam was lighting Los Angeles from across the Mojave Desert. North of the United States–Canada border, Winnipeg harnessed the power of the Nelson River before it emptied into Hudson Bay. In the Southwest, the Bureau of Reclamation finished Glen Canyon Dam on the Colorado River in 1962, inspiring Edward Abbey's fierce and funny novel *The Monkey Wrench Gang* (1975) about efforts to derail the operations of massive energy-production projects.

As the plot of *The Monkey Wrench Gang* informs its readers, city folks also power up their all-electric houses and run their factories with the help of far-distant strip mines and coal-burning power plants. A lot of Queensland has gone up in smoke to power Chinese, Korean, and Japanese factories. A lot of Wyoming has gone up in smoke on behalf of American lightbulbs and electric stoves. Carried by huge trains that stretch miles across the landscape, Wyoming coal has fueled the steam plants that keep student computers humming at Midwestern universities and traffic lights cycling red and green in Dallas, Houston, and Austin.

Moviegoers around the world know the landscape of Monument Valley from countless western film classics. Not far away, a huge strip-mining operation on Black Mesa in the early 1970s powered the Navajo Generating Station that shipped electric power to Phoenix and Los Angeles. As his eco-activist characters are deciding how best to foul up the works, Abbey includes both a concise summary of the operation and an extended jeremiad:

> All this fantastic effort—giant machines, road networks, strip mines, conveyor belts, pipelines, slurry lines, loading towers, railway and electric train, hundred-million-dollar coal-burning power plant...for what? All that for what? Why to light the lamps of Phoenix suburbs not yet built, to run the air conditioners of San Diego and Los Angeles, to illuminate shopping center parking lots at two in the morning.

Water does work for cities at a distance when it generates electricity, but it also needs to be brought into town. Industrializing cities have reached into their hinterlands for water since Philadelphia built the first steam-powered municipal waterworks in North America on the Schuylkill River in 1822. New York tapped the Croton watershed of Westchester County in 1842, the occasion for a grand civic celebration. Located on the dry margin of the Great Plains, the major cities of Colorado have reached into and tunneled under the Rocky Mountains. In contrast, Melbourne and Sydney, on the relatively rainy eastern edge of Australia, built sets of smaller nearby dams and reservoirs.

Cities that depend on deep wells have special problems. Weak land use regulations may allow well fields too close to industries that contaminate ground water, as in Miami. Much of Mexico City is built on a dry lake bed. Wells pump out the ground water, and land dries and collapses on itself, and parts of the city were sinking by five or more inches per year in the 2010s. Water supply also becomes a local planning issue when it pits environmentalists against development of new subdivisions that pave over land where the free percolation of rain water is vital for groundwater recharge—an added problem in Mexico City and a concern in San Antonio, Texas, and numerous other cities.

To control water is to determine the value of real estate and the future of industries, especially in arid regions like the American Southwest. When something is scarce, it is valuable. And when it is valuable, it is corruptible, a truth that drives the screenplay for the film *Chinatown* (1974), which condenses and dramatizes the most famous episode of North American water politics—the acquisition of water from the Owens Valley on the east side of the Sierra Nevada for Los Angeles. It is a story of municipal ambition, engineering hubris, and complicity on both sides—imperial Los Angeles had Owens Valley partners. For urban planning, the city's control of abundant water allowed it to annex the broad agricultural San Fernando Valley, setting the stage for massive suburbanization after World War II that created, like, the awesome habitat for Valley Girls.

Sustainable and regenerative cities

Cities invest dearly to obtain water, and they can still run out. Prolonged drought in 2017–18 left the reservoirs that supply Cape Town nearly empty and the city perilously close to "day zero," when the taps would run dry. Cape Town's crisis raises the so-called three E's of sustainability—economy, environment, and equity. The division of responsibilities between national and state governments controlled by different political parties, plus the unglamorous nature of infrastructure upkeep, meant that funds were not allocated to expand storage capacity to match a growing metropolis of four million. The system depends precariously on an annual rainy season to refill those mountain reservoirs, a pattern that may become uncertain with climate change. The countdown highlighted unequal water service in a city with deep economic and racial differences. Day-zero rhetoric and stringent consumption targets (down to 50 liters per person per day in January 2018) helped to convince middle-class households to cut back while angering low-income residents who saw both class and racial bias in water availability and mobilized around the slogan "Water for all or the city must fall." In fact, Cape Towners cut per capita consumption from 200 liters per day to 125, compared to the American average of 340. Returning rains relieved the Cape Town crisis but the mismatch between growing metropolis and precarious supply remained. São Paolo experienced the same trajectory a few years earlier; the sources of water shortfall were different but the political fallout was similar.

A water crisis is a challenge and opportunity to increase urban sustainability. Planners approach sustainability by looking for ways for cities to reduce their ecological footprint, meaning the resources that they use and consume to maintain and grow. Water use, for example, should not exceed the normal replacement of supply over the course of a year. In the current era of changing climate, those baselines are shifting. Cities depending on high mountain snowpack to fill reservoirs may need to reduce expectations of continued growth. Prolonged droughts like those that hit Mexico City in 2009–11, São Paolo in 2014–16, Cape Town in 2017–18, multiple Australian cities in the Millennium Drought of 2003–12, and multiple California cities in 2012–17 force a full menu of responses. A city can look for alternative supplies, like desalination plants for Sydney, Melbourne, Adelaide, and Perth. It can also try to reduce freshwater demand with permanent measures that go beyond emergency limits on lawn watering and car washing. Desert cities can promote xeriscaping, the replacement of water-hungry grass and shrubs imported from humid climates with indigenous vegetation adapted to aridity. There are multiple options for reusing "gray water" from washing and fully treated water from sewage treatment plants—thirsty golf courses are prime candidates.

Much sustainability planning centers on reducing demand for fossil fuels and substituting locally sourced solar power. The former requires changes in individual behavior and new building standards that prioritize energy efficiency. Promotion of local photovoltaic electricity requires support from zoning codes through sunlight access regulations that limit building heights and mandate setbacks. The details of building regulation, incentives, and zoning to facilitate renewable and distributed energy production via rooftop solar photovoltaic panels will be different in every city, but the trend is clear, with Australian and European cities as leaders. One and a half million Australian households have rooftop photovoltaic panels to generate electricity, including a quarter of the houses in Perth. Freiburg, Germany, a center for solar energy research and manufacturing, has adopted a SolarRegion strategy with stringent energy requirements for new buildings. Although the purpose is more targeted, solar access zoning goes back to New York's 1916 zoning ordinance, which required skyscrapers to step back from the street line to allow sunlight to reach streets, creating Manhattan's distinctive ziggurat towers from the 1920s and 1930s.

Sustainable cities also attempt to shrink the fuel demand of transportation to improve air quality and combat global warming. The key goal in developed counties is to reduce the total mileage driven by the average individual, measured as vehicle miles traveled (VMT) per capita. Every measure that provides nonautomobile transportation options, from rail transit to walking, works to reduce VMT. So do land use regulations and choices that make compact and connected neighborhoods. Cities that are designed to be socially strong and healthy for individuals are also more sustainable cities. American, Canadian, European, and Australian cities have gradually become more dense since the 1990s. Higher population density is associated with a decrease in private passenger transportation energy use, with Houston at the one extreme and Hong Kong and Ho Chi Minh City at the other. Using Perth as the model, Australian researchers have calculated that a resident of a compact city that facilitates walking generates half the greenhouse gases, half the waste heat, and substantially less household and construction waste than a resident in an automobile-dependent city.

For future planning, it is important to note that it may not help to replace individual automobile use with thousands of on-demand automobiles roaming the streets as their drivers wait for pings. On-demand services pull riders from public transit, walking, and bicycling as well as from private cars. Evidence from New York suggests that these services clog streets, reducing travel speeds and increasing fuel use rather than speeding movement. The shift of retail commerce to on line shopping and household package delivery adds to net congestion and fuel use. Meanwhile, fewer people die getting from one place to another in cities with high levels of public transit than in those that are auto-dependent.

Solar energy, water conservation, and reduction of automobile use are ways to "green" cities. Tree planting and river restoration are literal greening, steps in creating cities that are equally healthy for people, animals, and plants. Restoration of natural systems within cities is a step beyond sustainability with its measurement of net flows and orientation to the reduction of net inputs. Planners talk about biophilic cities where the natural environment is ever present, nearby, and accessible in a variety of forms, and regenerative cities in which living ecosystems support and restore biodiversity. These goals enter the planning process through broad policy plans that set a range of environmental goals and aim to coordinate actions across city departments dealing with parks, transportation, education, and community services in addition to land use and development. Oslo has a Green Structure Plan; Wellington is implementing a Biodiversity Strategy and Action Plan.

Cities are hot—not only as trend setters but as environments that capture and concentrate heat from the sun and from myriads of motors and furnaces. Brick and concrete absorb heat, and tall buildings slow the movement of air that can dissipate it. The result is an urban heat island, with thermometer readings at city center several degrees higher than on the fringe. The solution is to go green. Maintain green parks. Convert vacant lots into community gardens (the US term) and allotments (the UK term). Top buildings with living green roofs rather than composition shingles or tile. Plant trees and expand the city's tree canopy. Leafy neighborhoods are cooler than their asphalt jungle neighbors and offer the extra benefit of higher property values.

The city-state of Singapore has declared itself a "city in a garden" and made green a public priority. Tree planting and park connections increased the green area of the island from 36 percent in 1986 to 47 percent in 2007. The high-rise core is a model for ways to create green walls, green roofs, green balconies, and sky terraces. The National Library, opened in 2005 in the heart of the city, includes multiple gardens and a green sky courtyard. Public art extends the theme. Supertrees in the Garden by the Bay—featured in the film *Crazy Rich Asians*—are huge metal mushrooms or funnels festooned with greenery.

Clean, free-flowing water is another natural coolant. Many growing cities dealt with the inconvenience of natural streams by making them unnatural, lining their banks with concrete and burying them in culverts. Green cities look for ways to soften these hardened watercourses. Buried streams can be "daylighted," culverts beneath road crossings can be modified for fish passage, and concrete can be removed from river banks to allow vegetation to return. Birmingham (UK) has no rivers but has maintained 150 miles of free-flowing streams that wind through neighborhoods and linear parks. The Cheonggyecheon stream restoration in Seoul daylighted a stream once buried under an elevated highway. A six-mile stretch of the Los Angeles River—known to moviegoers as the concrete halfpipe featured in the chase scene in *Terminator 2*—is being returned to natural banks with green edges that can help to absorb rainwater. Like other green initiatives, these sorts of efforts are planning in a broad framework, involving coordination between transportation, land use, parks, and sewer and water agencies, often assisted by community organizations.

Trees and water together support the restoration of urban fauna from bees to birds to mammals. In the Pacific Northwest, opening urban streams assists the migration and survival of wild salmon, which once used entire river systems. Edmonton has created an engineering manual for designing roads with wildlife passages. Making cities safe for people and wildlife simultaneously is a cooperative process, often involving citizen activists and community groups along with government agencies, as with the other aspects of sustainability where professional land use planning is part of a larger effort. It also adds an additional demand on the programming of public open space. Planners who have long tried to balance demands for sports fields and formal flower gardens with desires for quiet picnicking and bird-watching now have to consider leaving areas completely undeveloped—quite a change from the profession's long-standing role in facilitating development.

Chapter 7
Unnatural disasters and resilient cities

Cities have been building walls again. In the nineteenth century, the modernizing cities of Europe outgrew the walls that had guarded against outsiders and controlled trade for centuries. Vienna replaced its wall with the broad *Ringstrasse* boulevard, and Brussels demolished its fourteenth-century wall to make its "small ring" road. Tallinn, Toledo, and Dubrovnik now sprawl beyond their fortified cores, leaving their picturesque walls and ramparts for the enjoyment of twenty-first-century tourists and filmmakers. Nanjing has preserved substantial segments of its historic wall while growing into a metropolis of eight million.

In recent decades, however, barriers have again arisen. Some protect city dwellers not against outsiders but from each other. Polarized cities are not simply segregated by ethnicity and religion. As planning theorist Scott Bollens notes, they can "contain a depth of antagonism and opposition beyond what the word 'divided' conveys," sometimes leading to violence that needs to be contained by physical walls.

Cities have also turned to physical barriers against natural forces. The Netherlands has long used dikes and pumps to push back the North Sea and create new land. River cities like Bangkok and New Orleans erect higher and higher levees for flood protection. Rising sea levels prompt massive public works to wall off London from the North Sea, Venice from the Adriatic, and Jakarta from the Sea of Java.

Walls and barriers raise complex issues of resilience: How can cities plan to prevent and mitigate social and political conflict? How can they plan for new environmental stressors from global climate change? Cities deal continuously with the incremental pressure of demographic and economic change that is the focus of most urban planning, but they also face abrupt disasters. Invading armies overrun cities, civil war turns them into combat zones, typhoons swamp them, and earthquakes shake them to rubble. All disasters are human disasters, either the direct result of human violence or "unnatural" results of people making themselves vulnerable to atmospheric and planetary instabilities.

Civil conflict

Cities are prime targets of terrorism and focal points in civil conflicts. Terrorism—the indiscriminate killing of ordinary citizens for a political purpose—lies at the middle of a spectrum of violent political acts that ranges from assassination and hostage taking to full guerrilla war against an occupying force. The US State Department definition is "pre-meditated politically motivated violence, perpetuated against noncombatant targets by subnational groups or clandestine agents, usually intended to influence a wider audience." The goals are to gain publicity for a cause, to raise costs to an oppressor, and eventually to bring political change. Terrorists target the symbols and representatives of economic and political power, and they try to bring pain and danger to centers of repressive power as when the Provisional Irish Republic Army (IRA) waged a bombing campaign in Manchester and London and when Chechen separatists attacked a Moscow theater.

Terrorists attack cities because they have a rich diversity of targets with concentrations of people in public places such as subways

(Madrid, London), shopping centers (Nairobi), hotels (Mumbai), sports arenas (Paris), tourist districts (Bali, Istanbul), and public squares (Ankara), and because they offer places for concealment. They house embassies and consulates that allow groups to indirectly attack a foreign power, as when Al Qaeda bombed the American embassies in Nairobi and Dar es Salaam in 1998. Regional communication centers like Istanbul and global communication centers like New York make attractive targets. Al Qaeda killed 213 and injured 4,000 at the US embassy in Nairobi but garnered limited attention in the United States. The response would have been much stronger to a similar attack in Tokyo or Paris.

The obvious physical planning response has been "defensive urbanism" by hardening potential targets and increasing surveillance of city centers. Cities can utilize license plate recognition and install closed-circuit TV cameras. They can close streets, establish checkpoints, and divert traffic with roadblocks. Britain established a "ring of steel" around parts of central Belfast in the 1980s and applied the same strategy to the city of London financial district after IRA bombings. Concrete barriers and checkpoints slow entering drivers to allow careful surveillance. Creating pedestrian-only areas and slowing all traffic by narrowing streets or reducing lanes are partial defenses against car bombs and vehicles used as direct weapons, but it is ultimately impossible to armor an entire city.

Internal walls are defensive urbanism carried to an extreme. They can reduce civil strife by separating hostile groups. They can also deepen conflicts by staking exclusive political claims to parts of a larger city. The Berlin Wall (1961–89) divided a culturally homogeneous city into political spheres. The physically unimpressive United Nations Green Line in Nicosia separated warring Greeks and Turks. Running through the heart of the city, the wall began as checkpoints under British authority and became a physical barrier after the Turkish occupation of northern Cyprus

9. Belfast Peace Lines are collections of relatively short barriers designed to reduce Catholic–Protestant confrontations and violence by blocking streets or separating volatile neighborhoods. Unlike earlier cities that were often surrounded by walls, in modern cities residents may find themselves separated from their neighbors by internal walls intended to reduce conflict or to enforce political and ethnic divisions.

in 1974 (although crossing restrictions relaxed after the southern Republic of Cyprus entered the European Union in 2004). Jerusalem's Green Line (1949–67) separated Jewish and Arab sectors and Arabs after the first Israeli–Arab war of 1948. The West Bank Barrier superseded it, shifting the line eastward to fragment Palestinian settlement areas in Jerusalem and the West Bank. War in Bosnia in the early 1990s split Christian Croats from Muslim Bosniaks along Mostar's central avenue, a dividing line enforced by military power during the war and social pressure after its end. Thirteen miles of peaceline walls separate Protestant and Catholic neighborhoods in Belfast, an intervention that helped cool three decades of violence known as the Troubles and remains part of the cityscape, damping down but not eliminating conflict. Belfast's ethnic landscape is too fragmented for a single wall; instead more than a dozen separate segments, built to specific requests rather than an overall plan, divide working-class Catholic and Protestant neighborhoods.

Planners in divided cities fall short if they attempt to be neutral and objective technicians. They fail to recognize the realities of ethnic difference if they practice "color-blind" planning. In Belfast, for example, efforts to assign residents to new housing without regard to religion ignored the practical necessity of maintaining separate Protestant and Catholic neighborhoods. Planners also ignored the different needs of Catholic areas with growing populations and Protestant areas in need of community stabilization. Israel has used legal and technical decisions to implement a political agenda, starting with a decision to substantially expand the jurisdictional area of Jerusalem, which turned controversial land use choices such as the expansion of Jewish neighborhoods into low-profile municipal decisions. Johannesburg's apartheid-based policies separated well-planned white districts and largely unplanned and underinvested black communities with tracts of open land, industry, and railroads. The post-apartheid city began to heal the gap by creating institutions for metropolitan planning and governance to explicitly link the disparate areas within single administrative structures.

More effective than simple regulations are efforts that tap the principles of equity and empowerment planning. Post apartheid Johannesburg was pulled between traditional centralized regulation that focuses on land use patterns and a newer style of community-based development focused on enhancing social and economic opportunity. In the South African context, development planning, with its emphasis on community participation and roots in the nonprofit service sector, diversifies the field and challenges traditional British approaches to town planning. On a smaller scale, the stable territorial bases of Nicosia's Greek and Turkish communities allowed local officials to cooperate on practical needs like a single sewer system and symbolic goals like restoration of the historic core on both sides of the line.

Avoiding "natural" disaster

We live on the surface of a world in constant motion and
vulnerable to the actions of earth, air, water, and fire. Our
atmosphere spawns gales, tornadoes, and huge tropical storms.
Rain turns rivers into surging floods, storm surge and tsunamis
devastate coastal communities, and climate change slowly alters
the same coastlines. Geological faults slip, continental plates grind
and shudder together, and volcanos erupt. Fires devour forests,
scrublands, and towns. Hazardous natural processes become
"natural disasters" when there are people in the way. An eruption
of Mount Vesuvius became a disaster because Romans built
Pompeii and Herculaneum within range of its lava and ashfall.
The hills above Malibu, California, are covered with oily brush
that has a natural burn cycle—not a big problem until the periodic
fires started burning the houses that movie stars (and others) built
in harm's way.

Land use planners have an obligation to consider how their work
sometimes creates communities that are vulnerable to these
events and how they can work to reduce potential harm. Their
contributions overlap with concerns of architecture and
engineering on the one hand and with the political choices for
disaster preparedness on the other. Some types of event are more
amenable to a planning approach than others. We know that
dozens of tornadoes are going to strike in the great central bowl of
North America every year, but we do not know when they will
occur or which small swath of land they will touch; they are
predictably unpredictable, happening regularly in time but
randomly in space. Individual households in Tornado Alley should
have storm cellars—remember what happened to Dorothy Gale
when she was caught outside by a Kansas twister and ended up
following a yellow brick road in the Land of Oz—but there is not
much that land use regulations can do to fend off their effects.
Floods are a different matter, recurring events that happen
irregularly but in predictable locations, repeatedly inundating the

same tracts of land and thereby giving planners a target for action. We can array other natural events—earthquakes, volcanic eruptions, typhoons—along the same dimensions of frequency and predictability of location. The Pacific Northwest has a BIG earthquake every few hundred years, but it is hard to know when the next one will come—an hour after I write this paragraph or a century from now.

Communities differ in vulnerability, which is the potential for damage, death, and disruption because of particular events. Vulnerability is the result of individual decisions to live in certain places (a seacoast) and to build in certain ways (a beach house is safer on deep pilings than on a concrete block foundation). It is also the result of cumulative social values and decisions that have brought sixteen million Floridians to live within twenty miles of the ocean. In turn, risk is the likelihood that a particular level of loss will be associated with a specific hazardous event. In effect, it is an actuarial concept derived from the interaction of vulnerability with likelihood of a dangerous or extreme event. Hurricanes hit the West Indies more frequently than New York, but the potential aggregate damage might be higher from a rare event like Hurricane Sandy because New York's population and invested capital make for great vulnerability.

Pro active antidisaster work has to deal with economic disadvantage. The more resources someone has, the better they can survive many types of disaster because they can get away if there is warning. In the nineteenth century, three cholera epidemics ravaged European and North American cities. After the 1849 epidemic arrived in New Orleans, Chicago newspapers chronicled its progress up the Mississippi to Natchez, Memphis, and St. Louis, with Chicago next. Richer residents had the warning to get out; poor people stayed and took their chances. When Hurricane Katrina hit New Orleans, the poorest neighborhoods and residents suffered the most because they were least able to flee and had fewer resources for sheltering in place.

The US Centers for Disease Control have a Social Vulnerability Index that uses fifteen variables to measure the ability of communities to respond to disasters and disease outbreaks. On a global scale, the earthquake that struck the very poor nation of Haiti in 2010 caused more than 100,000 deaths from direct effects and because of limited capacity for emergency services and reconstruction. A quake of comparable magnitude in Christchurch, New Zealand, the same year killed 185 people, and the city and nation had the resources to move quickly from devastation into recovery.

In the face of potential hazards, communities can try to build their way out of danger, or they can try to get out of the way. The construction option ranges from requiring quake-resistant construction to erecting massive dikes and sea walls. Getting out of the way involves limits on development in especially hazardous locations, meaning politically sensitive land use restrictions.

Earthquakes demonstrate difficulties with both approaches. We cannot prevent earthquakes, nor are tens of millions of people going to walk away from Santiago, Mexico City, Los Angeles, Tokyo, Athens, and other great cities in seismically active zones. Building codes that require new quake-resistant construction are a proven tool to reduce the impact of earthquakes, as is the retrofitting of bridges and other infrastructure to prevent collapse. However, strengthening unreinforced brick or stone buildings is challenging because of both expense and the large number of structures. The problem is acute in nations like Italy, Turkey, and Iran, where severe tremblors can level entire old towns. Limits on land uses are also problematic. Geologists know which parts of cities are built on dangerous slopes and unstable fill, but views or proximity to waterfronts make these areas valuable real estate. The heart of Mexico City lies on dried lake beds whose soil turns to jelly when shaken, as in the 1985 quake. There have been changes to building codes and some retrofitting of older buildings, but more than thirty million Mexicans living in the hazardous area suffered the effects of a second severe earthquake exactly thirty-two years later. In small, socially homogeneous, and government-friendly Christchurch, by contrast, new land use limitations have been adopted and accepted.

Water hazards come at different scales. Cities often flood temporarily when clouds drop five or seven inches of rain in a single day and the water pours off rooftops, paved streets, driveways, and parking lots, chokes storm sewers, and raises local streams. An obvious remedy is to replace hard surfaces with natural surfaces that can absorb the water. Cities can promote green roofs, repave parking lots with permeable surfaces, build retention ponds on vacant land, restore natural stream margins, and preserve wetlands—all measures to allow rain to soak into the ground rather than funneling into torrents. At the same time, the choice to protect a river city with higher and higher levees pushes flood waters toward less favored areas. On the middle Mississippi, part of the strategy to protect St. Louis from high water is to breach levees downstream, flooding farmland but relieving pressure on the city. New Orleans is protected with an even more elaborate system that includes a massive system of dams, levees, and spillways to divert part of a swollen river into a channel that bypasses the city and plans to dynamite levees below the city to flood a chunk of rural Louisiana. Poor people tend to live on the lowest land with the greatest likelihood of flooding, whether they are in the Lower Ninth Ward of New Orleans or marginal districts in Dacca, and they have the greatest likelihood of being sacrificed to save high-value districts and cities.

Houston, Texas, located on a flat Gulf Coast interlaced with bayous and streams, has devoted the last century to paving over more and more of its landscape and trying to engineer its way out of the resulting floods. Hurricane Harvey in 2016 dropped thirty-seven trillion gallons of water on southeastern Texas and overwhelmed drainage capacity, flooded more than two hundred thousand homes, and killed dozens of people. In response, residents have begun to change their approach. In 2018 they approved borrowing $2.5 billion for a combination of efforts to build out of danger with channel improvements and water retention basins and to get people and property out of the way of high water by buying out several thousand buildings in flood plains and acquiring land for permanent open space.

Climate change and urban futures

As global climate has warmed, wildfires have increased in size and intensity in North America and Australia—areas whose residents value rural and semirural living in forests and outback. On Friday, February 6, 2009, the premier of Victoria, Australia, warned that the next day would have the most dangerous fire conditions in the history of the state. Black Saturday, February 7, proved him right as a dozen major bush fires killed 180 people. A blazing forest engulfed Fort McMurray, Alberta, in 2016 and burned 2,400 buildings. Massive fire consumed nearly 7,700 homes and 260 commercial buildings in Paradise, California, in 2018 and killed at least 85 people. Changing climate with hotter, drier, and longer summers directly contributed to all of these disasters, as well as to devastating fires in Greece and Portugal.

Land use controls are weak tools when wildfires grow into massive firestorms, but limits on scattered development in dangerous areas make firefighting safer and more efficient. More than 30 percent of California housing lies in the wildland–urban interface where exurbs, resorts, and retirement communities are scattered among the trees. Transplanted urbanites are often unaware of fire dangers and ways to reduce risk until too late. Land use controls can limit the spread of small developments and individual homes into fire-prone environments. Oregon's land use system does this to good effect, but it is a hard sell in most states and provinces.

More discussion of the urban impacts of climate change has focused on water than on fire. Journalists and academics write books with titles like *Rising: Dispatches from the New American Shore, The Water Will Come: Rising Seas, Sinking Cities, and the Remaking of the Civilized World*, and *Extreme Cities: The Peril and Promise of Urban Life in the Age of Climate Change*. Reporters file innumerable stories about watery Miami and the slow drowning of Venice, with obligatory pictures of tourists wading knee-deep across Piazza San Marco. Earth scientists and climatologists try to balance the likelihood of gradual sea level rise against cataclysmic events like the collapse of the Greenland and Antarctic icecaps. Meteorologists weigh the extent to which warming oceans intensify tropical storms and document the way that rising seas exacerbate devastating coastal storm surge.

The same faith in public works behind flood-control dams and levees also fuels efforts to armor low coastlines. The Dutch have been doing it for centuries and with renewed investment after a disastrous North Sea storm and flood in 1952, so why not emulate them? The United Kingdom has a massive Thames Barrier to seal off the river from surging seas during peak storms. Venice hopes to complete a set of science-fiction pop-up barriers that are designed to seal off the three entrances to the city's lagoons during extreme weather; when finished in the early 2020s they are likely to give only a few decades of protection. The mouth of the Thames and Venice are relatively small and discrete sites, but what about armoring New York City? After the flooding from Hurricane Sandy, the city began to move forward with the Big U, a combination of levees, sea walls, and parks to protect lower Manhattan from a recurrence. The designers win points for including the "soft" element of parkland to absorb excess water, but the multi-billion-dollar scheme does not protect the other boroughs or the vulnerable cities of New Jersey and could leave them worse off by displacing high water. Contrast Boston's approach of neighborhood shore-based resilience that includes raising some parks and roads as barriers but also softening shorelines to allow greater absorption of high water. The city is pursuing the sorts of incremental investments that make sense when it is not known if sea levels will rise by two feet or eight feet in the next two generations.

Big projects are also tempting solutions in developing nations in Africa and southern Asia. Cities like Accra, Dhaka, and Manila are highly vulnerable. Eko Atlantic in Lagos is a new mini city on new land raised well above sea level; an eight-mile, twenty-five-foot sea wall will protect a planned three hundred thousand well-off residents from rising seas but do little for the thirteen million people in the rest of the city. Jakarta, a vast metropolis of thirty million, is threatened with drowning. In a city that is 97 percent paved, drainage channels and canals are often blocked, pumping stations are overwhelmed, coastal mangrove swamps are cleared for buildings, the city is sinking as groundwater pumping deflates its soil... and the Java Sea is rising. The government has protected the shore with a Coastal Wall that will only postpone the worst flooding for a decade or two, to be supplemented by the National Capital Integrated Coastal Development plan including a Great Sea Wall to close off the entire Jakarta Bay.

Technically sophisticated sea walls and barriers can capture public imagination and appeal to ribbon-cutting politicians, but they are enormously expensive stopgaps. Zoning to reduce or prohibit construction in flood-prone areas along rivers and coasts is cheaper and more effective, but also politically difficult. Owners of coastal properties repeatedly return to rebuild, trying to salvage the land value from damaged property. Vested development rights often override changes in land use plans. North Carolina in 2012 effectively ordered state agencies to ignore possible sea level change in land use planning even though the state's coastal counties have grown by 50 percent in population in twenty years. Residents in a dozen states during the 2010s built new housing in areas that are likely to be unlivable by 2050 at rates twice or even three times the rates in safer areas; the analysis pinpoints Norfolk, Charleston, and Corpus Christi.

Jakarta's problem may be daunting enough, but the greatest challenge that global warming will pose for city planning will surely be coping with climate refugees. Expected levels of climate change over the next several decades will alter rainfall patterns and disrupt agriculture and fisheries. The expectation is that people closer to the equator will find it harder to make a living and even to survive. Prolonged climate disruption in the Sahel region of western Africa has turned millions of Africans into migrants. Most have only been able to move short distances, but a fraction fueled the European migration crisis of the 2010s. Drought pushed 1.5 million Syrians into cities between 2006 and 2011, exacerbating the tensions that exploded into civil war. North America has yet to face similar situations, but cities in the northern states and Canada need to think about increased migration of destitute people as a problem for economic development, housing, and land use.

In the face of daunting global prospects, cities can take the lead in reducing greenhouse gas emissions. Mayors and civic leaders throughout the industrialized nations can act locally when national governments hesitate, working with organizations like C40 that brings together nearly one hundred mayors representing seven hundred million people. By 2019 emissions in London, Madrid, and Berlin had fallen more than 30 percent from peak levels and by a whopping 61 percent in Copenhagen. These gains are accomplished with familiar tools of transportation investments that encourage residents to reduce automobile use and green building standards that require energy-efficient buildings.

Resilience after disaster

Disasters are not a good opportunity for radically remaking a city. Architects and designers often see a devastated cityscape as the canvas for crafting an improved city. Christopher Wren, Robert Hooke, and John Evelyn drafted new street plans for London after the great fire of 1666, but none was implemented. Daniel

Burnham presented a comprehensive plan for San Francisco one month after the 1906 earthquake and fire. San Franciscans were too busy to pay attention, leaving the city as difficult to navigate now as a century ago. Berliners rebuilt after the devastation of World War II with the old street pattern. At root is the desperate need to get a city functioning again, with rebuilt housing and reopened businesses, combined with the inertia of real estate, since title to a piece of city land may be someone's last remaining asset. The social value of neighborhood and community is further reason why people tend to rebuild their cities as before.

Recovery from disaster involves four overlapping components. Emergency measures come first—search and rescue, debris clearance, temporary housing. Immediate action leads to the restoration of basic public services like water and electricity. As time and resources are available, authorities move to repair damaged roads and buildings. The more comprehensive reconstruction that follows may involve significant social and economic development, or it may reinforce the status quo.

Cities need to plan for resilience, which involves a myriad of efforts large and small, both physical and social, rather than dream about unlikely makeovers. The United Nations Office for Disaster Risk Reduction has a Making Cities Resilient program that offers suggestions in eight categories that span physical measures, organization, and institutional capacity. The latter is especially important because emergency assistance that arrives from the outside carries the agendas of the agencies and nongovernmental organizations that provide it and, especially in poorer countries, their arrogance. A study of hurricane relief across the Caribbean showed that top-down relief programs seldom delivered aid or undertook reconstruction that matched local needs. Instead, Philip Berke and Timothy Beatley found that "the principal resource available for recovery linked to long term development is the people themselves and their local knowledge and expertise." In effect, these findings are another vote for empowerment planning over reliance on top-down expertise.

Cities need to plan for small-scale disaggregated responses to disaster. The best comprehensive response plans will be at least partially inadequate and misconceived. Bureaucracies may be sluggish and unadaptive, as the Federal Emergency Management Administration was in New Orleans in 2005. Transportation and communication links may collapse as in Puerto Rico in 2017. It is easy to multiply examples from around the globe. Given the likelihood that top-down responses will fall short, cities need to decentralize for flexibility. They may design ways to isolate undamaged sections of water lines and power grid. They may encourage the formation of neighborhood action groups and shift responsibility for preparedness to community groups, as in Jamaica, or train the entire population at the local level as in Cuba, whose hurricane drills are a more comprehensive and sophisticated version of American civil defense drills from the 1950s. This sort of local self-reliance requires trust in everyday citizens. Elites often panic in civic emergencies, groundlessly fearing the unleashing of a mob. Ordinary folks cope with immediate mutual aid and cooperate with grassroots organizations for recovery. Proactive planning for resilience can strengthen these capacities through the tools of community development while promoting the disaggregated and localized access to services and facilities that is already good practice.

Kim Stanley Robinson's novel *New York 2140*, set in a future city that is half submerged by rising ocean levels, dramatizes the role of the self-organizing community. The book posits plenty of new technologies, like skyvillages suspended by blimps, but Robinson's unifying theme is resilience. The novel highlights the ever-present physicality and adaptability of a natural world ruled by weather and water. Tidal flows constrain everyday routines in the neo-Venice. Beavers colonize the new swamps in the Bronx and New Jersey, oyster beds have returned, and aquaculture helps feed the city. In effect, Robinson projects forward the insights of the ecologists, geographers, and environmental historians who are reemphasizing the functions of nature in and of the city. Robinson's New Yorkers also have the resourcefulness to craft new grassroots institutions—co-op buildings, neighborhood associations, and self-help groups that maintain the island's surviving skyscrapers. Residents improvise. Bureaucrats, first responders, and ordinary citizens all pitch in when a massive storm surge threatens the city. Robinson's future city revolves around the public sphere of debate and the messy but necessary work of working together to make things better.

So future New York may survive, like Tokyo after its 1923 earthquake and New Orleans after Katrina. So will its other peers. London, Beijing, and Singapore are unlikely to end as abandoned ruins. Unlike cities of antiquity, modern cities benefit not only from internal strength but also from the sometimes maligned global economy that allows them to draw resources from vast distances far more effectively than premodern places that succumbed to conquest or climate change. At the same time, global resources need to be used with local knowledge and community involvement. Violence-torn Belfast and storm-wracked New Orleans have needed the technical expertise of city planners, but reconciliation and reconstruction also require the participation and empowerment of the citizens who have to live with the results long after the experts have moved on.

Epilogue
Imagining future cities

Put two images side by side. For one, pick any of hundreds of artists' conceptions of future cities as forests of towering buildings. On the other side place a photograph of Shanghai's Pudong district skyline shimmering in the night. The two are hard to tell apart, raising the question of how planners and citizens should respond to the needs of the twenty-million-person city like Cairo and the twenty-five-million-person city like Shanghai. Compact cities that stretched across five or six miles in 1800 grew to the large metropolis of 1900 that stretched twenty miles and now to urban megaregions that may extend for two hundred miles. In this context, how best do we think about planning for the "environment-friendly, economically-developed, culturally-diversified and safe and livable city," to quote from the *Shanghai Master Plan 2017–2035: Striving for the Excellent Global City*?

Ask an acquaintance about cities of the future and you are likely to get two sorts of answers. Some respondents will go big, citing Buckminster Fuller's proposals for domed cities or Paolo Soleri's vision of cities as single megastructures housing hundreds of thousands of people. They'll rhapsodize about automated buildings, pneumatic transportation systems like hyperloops, and a future with an air car in every garage. Others will offer two words—*Blade Runner*—as shorthand for a long tradition of dystopian speculation. Look again, however, and see that the

10. Views of the new Shanghai skyline have become icons of headlong Asian urbanization in the same way that the New York and Chicago skylines symbolized the twentieth-century city. Shanghai's Pudong district has created a new center across the river from the older business district.

original *Blade Runner* makes a strong assumption about the continued social dynamism of future cities, an idea that reappears with surprising frequency in science fiction.

As cities and city planning move well into the twenty-first century, the challenge is to balance two prominent planning trends that are implied in the popular responses. We can call them Robot City and Human City. They seem completely different at first glance— even completely opposed. However, examples from present-day cities and ideas from speculative fiction suggest that we can and should blend the best of both approaches.

Robot City is big-data city, the city planned around the ability to gather and process vast amounts of real-time information for centralized control systems that regulate traffic flow, electricity use, and transit pricing. It is a hot market; at the 2018 Consumer Electronics Show in Las Vegas, more vendors displayed smart-city products than gaming products. The projected result is both a city full of mobile robots (including the smart self-driving cars that seem always around the corner) and, at least in science fiction, a city that is itself a giant artificial intelligence or stationary robot with a mind of its own.

Robot City is about holding the distant pieces together by helping the arteries and veins of the urban organism function more efficiently. Real-time data allow better and more efficient use of the wires that deliver electricity and the pipes that deliver water. People can move more rapidly on the same set of roads and tracks if instant data enable trains and vehicles to pack closely together. It is noteworthy that the first way that planners respond to urban megaregions is to attempt to improve transportation connections—true for China's Pearl River Delta and for England with its plans for "High Speed 2" rail from London to Midlands cities.

A city based on big data requires an array of fixed sensors, but it depends even more on the huge quantities of data generated by smart phones and by the businesses that depend on them. The data can have real-time impacts, like traffic cameras and GPS location data that might allow automatic adjustment of traffic signals to clear gridlock. It can also have long-term planning implications. In the United States, the distribution of Facebook "friends" can tell us which rural areas are oriented to which city. Ride- and car-sharing companies have a vast pool of data that would be greatly helpful for transportation planning—if they were willing to share it with city planners. Even so, the city of big data should be approached with caution because of privacy concerns. And just consider the traffic problems if the sky actually fills with self-driving flying cars and delivery drones. Los Angeles traffic snarls might seem tame in comparison.

Technologically futuristic cities are often conceived at large scale. In the early twenty-first century, nations in East Asia and the Middle East had enough mobile capital seeking an investment home to attempt entire new cities from the ground up. Saudi Arabia has floated a proposal for NEOM, a $500 billion city to be a global financial and technology center (the name comes from "neo" plus the first letter of the Arabic word for future). It will have skyscrapers and robots and green parks when and if built along the Red Sea in the nation's northwestern corner. In many cases, however, Robot City at the start of the 2020s was a dream more than reality. Songdo, Korea's "smartest city," has yet to live up to its potential. One hour from Seoul and near airport and seaport, it is supposed to be a smart and ecofriendly global business hub. It has smart city elements like pneumatic tubes to shoot garbage to a central facility, Internet-connected apartments, and water recycling, but is has been slow to attract residents because it lacks basic community services and connections that make a city livable. The idea did not work any better in Toronto, where Google's subsidiary Sidewalk Labs proposed to remake the waterfront as "a neighborhood built from the internet up," with a digital infrastructure so detailed that it will tell city workers when to empty trash cans. Initial enthusiasm waned when people began to wonder about the intensity of the surveillance required for it to work as advertised.

The second vision is a city planned at human scale and for environmental resilience. This is a planning vision that emphasizes both neighborhoods and nature. It embraces biophilic cities where natural systems of water, vegetation, and wildlife are preserved or restored within the metropolitan region and the ideas loosely grouped as "New Urbanism" that see the basic function of a city as bringing individuals together in small settings and communities. Its intellectual ancestors include big names of planning: Frederick Law Olmsted and Ebenezer Howard, who tried to find ways to integrate the natural environment into the industrial city at a walkable scale, as well as Jane Jacobs and her

11. Advertising posters for Fritz Lang's film *Metropolis* emphasized the verticality and monumentality of the urban future. Its imagery powerfully shaped the way we have imagined future cities.

concern for the ways that city dwellers utilize their cities day to day at the scale of the street, neighborhood, and park.

Robot cities make good cinematic backdrops—think of the air cars sweeping and swooping among the towers of globe-spanning Coruscant in *Star Wars* movies. Human cities are less exciting to put on screen. *Blade Runner* has come to epitomize popular conceptions of science fiction cities because it combines zippy technology, looming megabuildings, and a noir atmosphere borrowed from both *Metropolis* and *The Big Sleep*. Air cars dart among the towers and cop cars hover over the streets. Looking vaguely like 1940s radio-photograph consoles, the corporate ziggurats of the overworld dominate the cityscape. Flames inexplicably vent from the tops of towers. Searchlights zigzag the sky but fail to penetrate to the claustrophobic surface.

Take another look, however, and something else stands out. The film may be LA's "official nightmare," as Mike Davis has claimed, but this imagined city of 2019 is heterogeneous, disordered, and active. Taffey's Snake Pit, the bar visited by bounty hunter Ric Deckard, is dark, dangerous, but also intriguing. Women sport retro fashions, pipes are puffed and joints smoked, and masked dancers sway to techno-beat music. The bustling streets teem with vitality, the Asian faces suggesting its attractions for entrepreneurial immigrants. Many Los Angeles residents found the scene where Deckard grabs lunch at an outdoor market to be appealing rather than off-putting, and the entire pulsating mishmash of food carts, sushi bars, and discount retailers that line *Blade Runner* streets matches one of the standard twenty-first-century prescriptions for vitalizing bland American cities.

The film is a reminder that the essence—the essentials—of a city is not the physical container but the people it contains. Cities are where deals go down, ideas blossom, lovers arrange trysts, and conspirators hatch plots. Science fiction storytellers would be lost without the inescapable settings of the bustling marketplace and the crowded tavern—both places where a variety of goods and services can be found and where anybody can put in an appearance, meaning trouble and plot complications are just around the corner. The sociologist Peter Langer suggests that our understanding of cities oscillates between two metaphors—city as jungle and city as bazaar. Cities in both images are places of thick social relations, diversity, and constant motion. The urban jungle is intertwined, crowded, and marked by deadly competition for resources, but the city as bazaar "imagines the city as a place of astonishing richness of activity and diversity... a market, a fair, a place of almost infinite exploration and opportunity, a center of exchange."

In *Pedido Street Station*, British writer China Miéville imaged a city of New Crobuzon, whose residents enact the role of public space as articulated by design critics and social commentators like Richard Sennett, who argue that community identities are best formed, promoted, and defended in shared spaces. This is not passive observation by one of Walter Benjamin's *flaneurs* wandering the streets of Paris, but rather the creation of meaning by the active participation that is required for community life. Michel de Certeau in *The Practice of Everyday Life* argues that abstract plans do not create cities. Instead, myriad individuals generate the meaning of urban space by moving through it, using it, and filtering it through their own perceptions and imaginations in ways beyond control and discipline.

Readers quickly grasp that teeming New Crobuzon is a transfigured version of London—both the Victorian city and the late twentieth-century city in which Miéville grew up, spiced, he says, with bits of Cairo and New Orleans. We are in a made-up world that is the very opposite of Tolkien's Shire—urban, grubby, and complex rather than rural, cutesy, and socially one-dimensional. The map that accompanies the book resembles the top view of the cerebral cortex, perhaps to emphasize the role of the city as a place of constant information generation and exchange. The city is a rich amalgam of neighborhoods sorted by class, lifestyle, and species, but also under continual pressures of change. A typical apartment building houses a jumble of "petty thieves and steel workers and errand-girls and knife-grinders."

Birmin Zana, the Golden City of Wakanda in the film *Black Panther*, combines the technological and social visions. When seen from a distance, it looks like traditional futuristic towers in a park with extra snazzy transportation. Designer Hannah Beachler says, however, that she started with human interaction. The maglev transit system uses small shuttles that serve everyone equally, unlike the bus and rail systems in many American cities. They take inspiration from the privately operated tro tro minibuses of Ghana and the similar matatus of Kenya that are a cross between taxis and city buses. Pedestrians are thick on the streets, which are sites of bustling commerce. The Records Building is the center of the city to emphasize the continuities of community.

Observers of cities have long known that there is an informal social infrastructure of associations and places that foster trust and shared goals. "Third places" like cafes and bookstores are commercial establishments but also places to congregate, linger, and interact. Public and semipublic spaces like parks, schools, playgrounds, sidewalks, community gardens, farmers' markets, and flea markets are venues where people can assemble freely and, ideally, interact across lines of class, race, and age. Branch libraries are an example as vital sites of learning and self-help, community activities, and personal connections. Helsinki calls its new library a citizenship factory. Everyone except free market ideologues likes public libraries. As writer Zadie Smith writes in a defense of her branch library in London, "a library is one of those social goods that matter to people of many different political attitudes.... They are a significant part of our social reality."

City planning has to make it easy for the physical machinery of cities to function smoothly and to promote economic development and opportunity, but it also has a responsibility to protect and enhance the small-scale places and institutions that enrich daily life. Future cities will be better places to live when big data are used effectively for community needs. Most people like civic institutions where we can meet and interact even more than we like search engine algorithms. The challenge, which the best urbanists and futurists address, is to be smart about our goals for livable cities before we decide just how to make cities smart. Perhaps planning to give everyone easy access to a branch library is a good way to start.

References

Chapter 1: Streets and buildings

Laws of the Indies: English translation by Axel Mundigo and Dora Crouch reprinted by The New City with permission from "The City Planning Ordinances of the Laws of the Indies Revisited, I," *Town Planning Review* 48 (July 1977): 247–68.

Heather Robertson, *Grass Roots* (Toronto: James Lewis & Samuel, 1973), 39.

Comparative street patterns: https://geoffboeing.com/2018/07/comparing-city-street-orientations/

Manila: Thomas S. Hines, *Burnham of Chicago: Architect and Planner* (New York: Oxford University Press, 1974), 213, 207.

Chapter 2: The suburban solution

Jack London, *People of the Abyss* (London: Isbister and Company, 1903), ix.

Adna F. Weber, "Suburban Annexations," *North American Review* 166 (May 1898): 616.

Disraeli quote: Peter Jukes, *A Shout in the Street: An Excursion into the Modern City* (Berkeley: University of California Press, 1990), 10 [quoting Thomas Burke, *Streets of London*].

Douglas Coupland, *Shampoo Planet* (New York: Washington Square Press, 1992), 218.

William H. Whyte Jr., "Urban Sprawl," in *The Exploding Metropolis*, ed. the editors of *Fortune* (Garden City, NY: Doubleday, 1958), 134–35.

Chapter 3: Saving the center

Blight: Richard Nelson and Frederick Aschman, *Conservation and Rehabilitation of Major Shopping Districts*, Urban Land Institute Technical Bulletin No. 12 (Washington, DC, 1954), 5.

Ivan Allen, *Journal of Housing*, 23 (August 1966): 458.

Margaret Drabble, *The Ice Age* (New York: Knopf, 1977), 28.

Sinclair Lewis, *Babbitt* (New York: Harcourt Brace, 1922), 1.

Chapter 4: Contested communities

Margaret Drabble, *The Ice Age* (New York: Knopf, 1977), 25–26.

T. Coraghessan Boyle, *The Tortilla Curtain* (New York: Viking, 1995), 158–59.

Lisa Peattie, *Planning, Rethinking Ciudad Guayana* (Ann Arbor: University of Michigan Press, 1987), 16.

Leonie Sandercock, *Cosmopolis II: Mongrel Cities in the 21st Century* (New York: Continuum, 2003), 1.

John Stuart Mill, *Principles of Political Economy with Some of Their Applications to Social Philosophy*, 2 vols. (London: John W. Parker, 1848), 2:119.

Chapter 5: Metropolis and megaregion

E. H. Bennett, "Some Aspects of City Planning with General Reference to a Plan for Ottawa and Hull," *Addresses Delivered before the Canadian Club of Ottawa, 1914–1915* (Ottawa: Rolla L. Crain Co., 1915), 7.

Governor Tom McCall, Address to Oregon Legislature, January 8, 1973, https://digital.osl.state.or.us/islandora/object/osl:16802

Megaregion maps: https://www.citylab.com/life/2019/02/global-megaregions-economic-powerhouse-megalopolis/583729/

Chapter 6: Nature in the city

Alida Brill, "Lakewood, California: 'Tomorrowland' at Forty," in *Rethinking Los Angeles*, ed. Michael Dear, E. Eric Schockman, and Greg Hise (Thousand Oaks, CA: Sage, 1996), 107.

Edward Abbey, *The Monkey Wrench Gang* (New York: Harper Perennial, 2007), 173.

Chapter 7: Unnatural disasters and resilient cities

Scott A. Bollens, *City and Soul in Divided Societies* (New York: Routledge, 2012), 6.

Philip Berke and Timothy Beatley, *After the Hurricane: Linking Recovery to Sustainable Development in the Caribbean* (Baltimore: Johns Hopkins University Press, 1997), 185.

Epilogue

Peter Langer, "Sociology—Four Images of Organized Diversity," in *Cities of the Mind: Images and Themes of the City in Social Science*, ed. Lloyd Rodwin and Rob Hollister (New York: Plenum, 1984), 100–101.

Zadie Smith, *Feel Free* (New York: Penguin Press, 2018), 11–12.

Further reading

Visualizing cities

Barber, Peter. *London: A History in Maps*. London: Topographical Society of London, 2012.

Hayden, Dolores. *A Field Guide to Sprawl*. New York: Norton, 2004.

Knox, Paul. *Atlas of Cities*. Princeton, NJ: Princeton University Press, 2014.

Reps, John. *The Making of Urban America*. Princeton, NJ: Princeton University Press, 1965.

Solnit, Rebecca. Infinite Cities: *A Trilogy of Atlases—San Francisco, New Orleans, New York*. Berkeley: University of California Press, 2019.

History

Fishman, Robert. *Urban Utopias in the Twentieth Century: Ebenezer Howard, Frank Lloyd Wright, Le Corbusier*. New York: Basic Books, 1977.

Flint, Anthony. *Wrestling with Moses: How Jane Jacobs Took on New York's Master Builder and Transformed the American City*. New York: Random House, 2009.

Hall, Peter. *Cities of Tomorrow: An Intellectual History of Urban Planning and Design in the Twentieth Century*. 4th ed. New York: Wiley, 2014.

Hayden, Dolores. *Building Suburbia: Green Fields and Urban Growth: 1820–2000*. New York: Vintage, 2003.

Hurley, Amanda Kolson. *Radical Suburbs: Experimental Living on the Fringes of the American City*. Cleveland: Belt Publishing, 2019.

Isenberg, Alison. *Downtown America: A History of the Place and the People Who Made It*. Chicago: University of Chicago Press, 2004.

Ladd, Brian. *Ghosts of Berlin: Confronting German History in the Urban Landscape*. Chicago: University of Chicago Press, 1997.

Sen, Siddhartha. *Colonizing, Decolonizing, and Globalizing Kolkata: From a Colonial to a Post-Marxist City*. Amsterdam: Amsterdam University Press, 2017.

Spain, Daphne. *How Women Saved the City*. Minneapolis: University of Minnesota Press, 2001.

Urban form and urban design

Barnett, Jonathan. *Redesigning Cities: Principles, Practice, Implementation*. New York: Routledge, 2017.

Calthorpe, Peter, and William Fulton. *The Regional City: Planning for the End of Sprawl*. Washington, DC: Island Press, 2000.

Duany, Andres, Elizabeth Plater-Zyberk, and Jeff Speck. *Suburban Nation: The Rise of Sprawl and the Decline of the American Dream*. New York: Farrar, Straus and Giroux, 2000.

Gehl, Jan. *Cities for People*. Washington, DC: Island Press, 2010.

Jacobs, Allan B. *Great Streets*. Cambridge, MA: MIT Press, 1993.

Speck, Jeff. *Walkable Cities: How Downtown Can Save America, One Step at a Time*. New York: Farrar, Straus and Giroux, 2012.

Communities

Massey, Douglas, and Nancy Denton. *American Apartheid*. Cambridge, MA: Harvard University Press, 1993.

Medoff, Peter, and Holly Sklar. *Streets of Hope: The Fall and Rise of an Urban Neighborhood*. Boston: South End Press, 1999.

Nightingale, Carl. *Segregation: A World History of Divided Cities*. Chicago: University of Chicago Press, 2012.

Rothstein, Richard. *The Color of Law: A Forgotten History of How Our Government Segregated America*. New York: Liveright, 2017.

Sandercock, Leonie. *Towards Cosmopolis: Planning for Multicultural Cities*. New York: Wiley, 1998.

Sandoval-Straus, Andrew. *Barrio America: How Latino Immigrants Saved the American City*. New York: Basic, 2019.

Talen, Emily. *Neighborhood*. New York: Oxford University Press, 2019.

Transportation and environment

Beatley, Timothy. *Green Urbanism*. Washington, DC: Island Press, 2000.

Cervero, Robert. *Beyond Mobility*. Washington, DC: Island Press, 2017.

Downs, Anthony. *Still Stuck in Traffic: Coping with Peak-Hour Traffic Congestion*. Washington, DC: Brookings Institution, 2004.

Gottlieb, Robert, and Simon Ng. *Global Cities and Urban Environments in Los Angeles, Hong Kong, and China*. Cambridge, MA: MIT Press, 2017.

Newman, Peter, Timothy Beatley, and Heather Boyer. *Resilient Cities: Overcoming Fossil Fuel Dependence*. Washington, DC: Island Press, 2017.

Pelling, Mark, and Sophie Blackburn. *Megacities and the Coast: Risk, Resilience and Transformation*. New York: Routledge, 2014.

Sadik-Khan, Janette, and Sete Solomonow. *Street Fight: Handbook for an Urban Revolution*. New York: Wiley, 2016.

Spirn, Ann Whiston. *The Granite Garden: Urban Nature and Human Design*. New York: Basic Books, 1984.

Disaster and resilience

Bohl, Charles C., David Godschalk, Timothy Beatley, Philip Berke, David Brower, and Edward J. Kaiser. *Natural Hazard Mitigation*. Washington, DC: Island Press, 1999.

Bollens, Scott. *City and Soul in Divided Societies*. New York: Routledge, 2012.

Klinenberg, Eric. *Palaces for the People: How Social Infrastructure Can Help Fight Inequality, Polarization, and the Decline of Civic Life*. New York: Crown, 2018.

Savitch, Hank. *Cities in a Time of Terror: Space, Territory, and Local Resilience*. Armonk, NY: M. E. Sharpe, 2008.

Solnit, Rebecca. *A Paradise Built in Hell: The Extraordinary Communities That Arise in Disaster*. New York: Viking, 2009.

Vale, Lawrence, and Thomas Campanella, eds. *The Resilient City*. New York: Oxford University Press, 2004.

Megacities and future cities

Abbott, Carl. *Imagining Urban Futures: Cities in Science Fiction and What We Might Learn from Them*. Middletown, CT: Wesleyan University Press, 2016.

Campanella, Thomas. *The Concrete Dragon: China's Urban Revolution and What It Means for the World*. New York: Princeton Architectural Press, 2011.

Du, Juan. *The Shenzen Experiment: The Story of a Chinese City*. Cambridge, MA: Harvard University Press, 2020.

Glaeser, Edward. *Triumph of the City*. New York: Penguin, 2011.

Graham, Stephen. *Vertical: The City from Satellite to Bunker*. New York: Verso, 2016.

Hamnett, Stephen, and Belinda Yuen, eds. *Planning Singapore: The Experimental City*. New York: Routledge, 2019.

Silver, Christopher. *Planning the Megacity: Jakarta, Indonesia in the Twentieth Century*. New York: Routledge, 2011.

Sims, David. *Understanding Cairo*. Cairo: American University in Cairo Press, 2012.

UN Habitat. *Urbanization and Development: Emerging Futures*. Nairobi: United Nations Human Settlements Program, 2016.

City Planning

Index